Letting Go
With Love:
The Grieving
Process

Other Books by Nancy O'Connor, Ph. D.

How To Grow Up When You're Grown Up:
Achieving Balance in Adulthood

How to Talk to Your Doctor

Endorsements for
Letting Go With Love: The Grieving Process

You have done unbelievable GOOD for people. God bless you. You have changed so many people's lives with your book. Thank you for all your have done for my people and myself.

Teresita Tinajero, Director Instituto de Tanatology de Mexico

Mexico City, DF

Letting Go With Love: The Grieving Process A counselor shares her experiences with bereavement and the stages of the grief process in a reassuring self-help book that will be valuable to teenagers and adults dealing with loss.

Booklist: American Library Association

This book makes for comforting reading. For someone who has never known the sadness and loneliness of death, it offers encouragement, advice, and hope in small palatable doses.

The Mail Tribune, Medford Oregon

Letting Go With Love offers a resource for those in the midst of grief; for those anticipating a death including their own, and for those emotionally hampered by unresolved grief that has lingered for many years.

Arizona Senior World

Letting Go With Love:
The Grieving Process

by

Nancy O'Connor, Ph.D.

Acknowledgment is made to Medic Publishing Company and Amy Hillyard Jensen for permission to reprint the material in Appendix A, and to Concern for Dying, 250 W. 57th Street, New York City, NY 10107 for permission to reprint "The Living Will."

Copyright ©2007
by Nancy O'Connor, Ph.D.
All rights reserved

Printed in the United States of America

Second Revised and Enlarged Edition 2007

ISBN: 978-0-9613714-8-7
SANS Number 676-2607
10-9-8-7-6-5-4-3-2-1
First Printing

La Mariposa Press
1990 E. Campbell Terrace, Arizona 85718-5952
Phone: 520-615-1244
Fax: 520-299-4840
Web site: www.lamariposapress.com

Cover Design: Zorbabel Leon

ACKNOWLEDGEMENTS

This book would not have been possible without the cooperation, encouragement, and support of other people. I want to thank Tanya Jarvik for her brilliant editorial work.

Many people facilitated my personal growth and professional interest in grief work. Significant among these are Drs. Frances Scott and Saul Toobert of the University of Oregon. Their creative teaching went far beyond the traditional academic format: their students learned not only intellectually, but also grew emotionally and personally.

Over the years, many clients have been teachers for me. They have given me their trust in knowing that I care and respect them in times of need.

I am grateful to Jan Ripberger, who typeset the manuscript.

I wish to thank The Instituto Mexicano de Tanalologia in Mexico City, its founder Teresita Tinajero, and her excellent staff for using my book to teach students about issues in death, dying and the grieving process. Thanks also to my Spanish publisher, Editorial Trillas S.A, and my editor there, Priscila Harfush-Melendez.

Finally, I wish to thank Dr. Elisabeth Kubler-Ross for taking time in her busy schedule to review the manuscript and to endorse the book.

DEDICATION

To all the people who have come into my life and left again. To those who have loved me and allowed me to love them. Through these relationships I have learned, grown and grieved their loss. Some were lengthier than others and emotionally mixed with joy and pain, especially my relationships with my parents, my grandparents, my siblings and most of all my infant daughter, Mary Margaret, who died when she was just two days old.

TABLE OF CONTENTS

PREFACE TO THE SECOND EDITION by Saul Toobert, Ph.D.

When Nancy O'Connor was a doctoral student, she was part of our team at the University of Oregon Gerontology Center that produced *Confrontations of Death*, an experiential course founded by the Center's Director, Frances G. Scott, to sensitize the gerontology students about issues of death and dying likely to occur in their older client populations. Dr. O'Connor was an instructor in gerontology and a T-group facilitator for many of the groups that comprised this course. The course became famous on the campus and spread to other universities around the nation. Unlike most university courses, which are a "head trip," this course was concerned with students' feelings as well as thoughts. Dr. O'Connor's interest in the field of grief likely was affected by her studies of gerontology and her participation in this course. *Letting Go With Love* is an important book in the field. It includes an insightful, readable description of the grieving process. It is a perceptive account of the issues of grief by an author who has experienced grief more than once and who has worked with many grieving clients. The grief process is poignantly described and responses to loss are discussed with reference to situational variations. Dr. O'Connor's observations and examples are interesting and helpful to the reader who may be in grief. Grief is seen as a normal response to loss. O'Connor inductively moves us from specific occurrences to the griever to the reasoned general principles in the process. She deals sensitively with responses to differing losses such as death of children, parents, spouses, suicide and loss by miscarriage, abortion and adoption. She also deals with grief as it relates to society's exclusion of the illicit or same gender relationship. This is a discerning treatise that will be appreciated both by the griever and for the hypotheses it offers the researcher.

INTRODUCTION

WHAT THIS BOOK IS ABOUT: WHAT IT CAN DO FOR YOU

When people die, their suffering is over, at least in life on earth. But those who are still living are faced with huge pressures, devastating trauma, important decisions, and powerful emotions. The survivors' suffering or grieving has just begun. The attention of friends and relatives has been focused on the one who was dying. But now the ones most closely affected by the death need the concern and caring of family and friends.

Most of us don't know what grief will be like until we experience it firsthand. We expect to be sad and hurt, but we may be surprised to feel other emotions, such as anger and guilt. We may discover that after someone dies, our relationships with others change. Our families and friendships may not be the same because of the changes we undergo after a loss.

In recent years, research has shown that there are identifiable patterns of emotions in grief. Knowing what those are can help you recognize that the turmoil and pain you feel are part of healing the injury that death has inflicted.

When a person can deal successfully with change, he or she can reach a higher level of growth, sensitivity and understanding of self and others. The death of someone important in our lives is a change: a major one, and sometimes a sudden one. But change, even painful change, is an important, necessary part of being alive.

Loss of someone through death is a particularly painful change, especially if you felt deep love toward that person. The more intense and deep your love, dependence, and hopes are, the more it will hurt to lose her or him.

There's no getting around the pain; you must get through it. You can't avoid it; you must become truly alive to your emotions. Avoiding the emotions of grief is a dangerous business that can lead to illness and serious distress. Worst of all, not dealing with our emotions leaves us psychologically stuck, unable to change and grow. Continuing to dwell on the anger or depression or guilt that arises during grief would be like having an open cut on your skin that continues to bleed and leaves the injured flesh exposed. Not only does the wound never heal, but eventually infection sets in and leads to worse problems.

So it is with grief. Progress in healing happens gradually, but eventually it is completed. If healing is blocked, infection, in the form of emotional damage, arrested growth and inability to live life fully, takes over.

Healing is accomplished by *grief work.* It's work because you can't approach it passively; you have to manage it. You will sometimes feel pain and resistance. At times you think that you'll never recover from this loss. But by doing the work experiencing, expressing and managing the emotions that you feel, you *will* recover. You'll be able to move on from the past, to live in the present and envision the future.

Surviving grief doesn't mean that you no longer miss the one who died. That person is in your life forever, but his role in your life must change. You can continue to love him or her, but the love eventually becomes a smaller part of your life. You must say the final goodbye so that you can move on. You must let him go with love.

I came to write this book after of many years of experience as a counselor and a human being. My own life has contained a number of losses. My father committed suicide when I was a young woman. I had a baby who died. I have said goodbye to dear friends who died from accidents or illness. And, while I was writing this book, my mother died after several years of failing health.

Since the first edition was published, three of my four siblings have died. I've also experienced loss through divorce, moving, watching my children grow up and other personal and professional changes.

In counseling people who are grieving for their own losses, I've been able to draw on my experiences to assure them that others have felt the same kinds of pain and that one *does* survive. I've learned much from my clients about suffering and surviving. Now I'd like to share that knowledge and understanding with you.

People going through grief have some things in common, such as the stages of the grief process. The first three chapters cover these universal experiences. The material in these chapters can help you with any grieving situation, whether this is a death in your own life, or when a friend has a loss, or when you are faced with a change through illness, separation or financial crisis.

The next two chapters go into more detail about specific losses. Although grieving follows a predictable pattern, the experience of losing a wife after fifty years of marriage is not the same as the death of a friend or a teen-aged child. Each chapter looks at some of the special problems connected with specific losses, while also containing material that may apply in other situations.

The chapter on death of the self is written to offer aid to those who have a terminal illness, or to those close to someone who must face death soon. Another chapter looks at the unique circumstances facing the survivors of a suicide.

The next two chapters are meant to help you recognize the patterns in your life that may influence how *you* process grief. You can identify your own ways of coping with change and use this knowledge to heal yourself and to choose to continue living. The most important thing I can tell you is that you *can* choose. Life can go on in a rich, exciting way – *you* are the one who has the power to make it happen.

This second edition has been moderately revised, and I have included two new chapters at the end of the book. These have been added to illuminate issues we are now dealing with in our modern lives – specifically, catastrophic deaths and care-giving.

You may decide to read only parts of this book right now, especially if you're groping for ways to handle a particular recent loss. You may find there are parts you'll come back to later. You may even find sections you don't understand or don't believe. But later those ideas will mean more to you, when you have moved from one stage of grief to another. The book can help you be better prepared for deaths in the future or to complete your grief for a long-ago death that you may never have released.

My wish is to help you understand your process as you grieve, to realize that grief has a progressive course and to assist in knowing that through all your current pain *you will survive* and, in time, once more experience joy in living.

Emotional reactions to the death of a loved one follow a fairly defined course. By giving in to these feelings and letting them occur in their natural timing, and being aware of things you may do that block the process, healing will take place. Death is a wound – a severe and painful psychological wound. As with any injury to the physical body, healing requires tender loving care, gentleness, and time.

Grieving is all the feelings, reactions and changes that occur during the process of healing. You have a choice in how you will heal yourself, although it may not feel like a conscious choice in the beginning. One choice is to allow yourself to grieve, to feel all of the anguish and fear and pain as they present themselves to you. This is the choice that eventually allows you to go on with your life.

The other choice is a move toward non-feeling, toward your own psychological death and eventually toward your physical death. Previous grieving patterns and individual personality traits contribute to the way you will naturally react to bereavement in the beginning. These are your natural predispositions, but you *can* change if old patterns do not serve you well.

What's most important in learning to live with loss is letting yourself feel. Allow! Allow! Allow! Allow yourself to feel – to experience – to live again.

To fear death, gentlemen, is nothing other than to think one wise when one is not; for it is to think one knows what one does not know. No man knows whether death may not even turn out to be the greatest blessing for a human being; and yet people fear it as if they knew for certain that it is the greatest of evils.

- Socrates

CHAPTER ONE

WHEN SOMEONE DIES

We live in a death-defying and death-denying society. We fight and resist death; we hurry through our mourning and rush to get back to "normal." This attitude makes the grieving process more difficult and confusing for the survivors because it denies the importance and depth of their feelings.

Not so long ago, death was experienced as a natural part of the life cycle. Most people died at home surrounded by family and friends. Children were around the dying process and included in the funeral and burial rituals.

Today, many of our efforts to prolong life or minimize grieving emotionally shortchange everyone involved. This can leave us with unresolved pain.

The Depersonalization of Dying

Over sixty percent of us die in institutions such as hospitals and nursing homes. With the advances of modern

1

medicine and the "heroic" measures available to extend life, most people are whisked off to the nearest hospital emergency room and turned over to strangers to be shocked, monitored, punctured, poked, and pounded by intimidating pieces of machinery while they are dying. Family and friends are not only excluded from the presence of the loved one; they often are denied the right to make decisions about what measures are to be taken to continue life. Nor is the dying person consulted or advised of what is being done.

Death is viewed as an enemy to be conquered at all costs, rather than a natural, inevitable part of being human, being alive.

After death, the body is taken to a mortuary or funeral parlor where strangers embalm, dress, perfume, and make it up with cosmetics to give the appearance of life. More denial.

By contrast, in the late 19th century less than twenty percent of Americans died in hospitals. The common occurrence was for people to die in the home where they had lived most of their lives. People often knew when they were dying, unless death was caused by an accident or sudden illness. The dying person had a chance to finish the emotional business of his or her life in familiar surroundings. In the last hours, vigilant family members and friends circled around to say goodbye.

Not all deaths were expected, then or now. Life before advanced medical technology also included many sudden, untimely deaths. Prized animals were slaughtered for food. Babies and young children died of childhood diseases or accidents. Women died in childbirth; men were killed in wars and accidents.

After the death, family members took care of the burial. The women washed and dressed the body, while the men made the casket and dug the grave. What a wonderful opportunity to complete obligations to the departing family member and to come to terms with the finality of the person's life – and to say goodbye with love and care!

The body was often buried on the grounds of the home, where survivors would continue to regard the dead person as part of their environment. During the first days after the death, friends and neighbors brought food and support for the mourners.

In the old, rural way of death and mourning, the close involvement of each family member with the dying one helped survivors to view death as natural and accept it as part of the life cycle. Not a strange and horrible occurrence, but a part of life. Unfortunately, we have lost the personal contact in the death rituals.

Our cultural denial of death began to grow as people moved to cities to work in factories. Hospitals became a place to go to seek cures. The medical profession began to view death as a failure, and stepped up efforts to fight the "enemy" of death with increasingly sophisticated technology such as drugs, surgery and machinery. These prolong the last days or months of life, even though the survivor is often semi-conscious, unconscious, even brain dead much of the time.

As more people went to hospitals, their impending death was greeted with denial, first by the medical staff, then by their families. The dying person began to view death as the enemy and to struggle against it. The fight to live in the face of impossible odds has always been the last battle lost. The final failure! The truth is that death isn't a failure. It is the natural and inevitable end of life. Something we all must face.

Communication between the dying loved one and family members changed. Truth was changing. In an attempt to "spare the feelings" of the dying person, lies crept into the dying process. Doctors lied, nurses lied, family members lied and eventually the dying person lied. The subject became taboo, veiled in secrecy and deceit. Everyone began to pretend that death was something unreal, an illusion. Relatives no longer keep watch by the person's bedside, but come according to hospital or nursing home visiting hours.

Most people fear dying alone or among strangers, unloved and uncared for. We also fear being dependent or undergoing intolerable pain, falling, choking or suffocating to death. With the prevailing denial of death among families, these are reasonable fears, especially for the lonely people living alone, residents of nursing homes or the seriously ill person in a hospital bed, wondering when her loved ones will come again to visit.

In an attempt to reverse this trend of death in unfamiliar surroundings, the Hospice Movement was started in England in the 1960's, and is gaining popularity in the United States. The Hospice principle advocates dying at home, again surrounded by family members. The staff provides support and information to the entire family; they encourage open, honest communication. They also believe in reasonable pain control, so that the dying person can be as comfortable as possible to the end.

In the United States, Hospice care is paid for by most major insurance companies when ordered by a physician, so long as the dying person has six months or less to live. These programs are so popular that most cities have several of them. If you are interested, call your local city or county health department to see if there is one in your community. Many include both in-home and hospital care. They always need compassionate volunteers.

With our busy lives, greater mobility, and separation from family members, death is no longer a part of our lives. Even if a member of the family is soon to die, it is not part of the day-to-day reality for a son or daughter who lives 2,000 miles away. The distant child or sibling doesn't participate in the imminent death and may feel it is happening to someone else, a stranger. They may attend the funeral but it has a touch of unreality and lacks true connectedness.

Nonetheless, a funeral brings the idea of death uncomfortably close. When we see, or are involved in some way with, another person's dying, we experience a sense of loss of ourselves. We start to think of our own future death. We mourn for the deceased one and for ourselves. Part of the intensely strong feelings and confusion experienced during the grieving period comes from these mixed emotions: of missing the other person, and at the same time, being glad it is he or she who is dead, not I.

This same self-consciousness is why friends and neighbors are often uncomfortable expressing their condolences to those who have recently lost a loved one. Subconsciously, they are glad they are not going through the pain of losing someone important to them. In watching someone else's grief, they are forced to imagine themselves in a similar situation, to think of how it would be to lose a parent, spouse, or child. They also may begin to think of the limits of their own lives. They may be sincerely sympathetic, but they feel guilty for being glad that it is not their loss. These conflicting emotions are a natural part of thinking about death. Recognizing them can help you deal with a friend's mourning or your own.

Denying Our Emotions

The taboo of talking about death in our country has far-reaching implications for the dying, as well as for the survivors. Those nearing the end of their lives are cheated of completing unfinished business in relationships, such as saying goodbye, and asking for or bestowing forgiveness for perceived wrongs during their lives. It is most difficult to accomplish these necessary tasks if the one you are trying to talk to responds to your efforts by saying, "Now, you are not going to die. I don't want to hear another word."

Denying death may seem to be a way of easing our grief, but in fact it has the opposite result. When we deny dying, we also deny an important part of authentic living. Death is a natural consequence of living. No one escapes it. Life is full of a variety of experiences for all of us. We have good times and bad times. Times of sadness, disappointment, frustration, and sorrow, as well as times of joy, love and happiness. Death is just another experience. But because it is unknown, it is riddled with fear.

Most of us seek happiness and avoid painful or negative feelings. We live in the foggy myth that happiness is the only acceptable state of existence. The French philosopher Philippe Aries notes that it has become the "moral duty and social obligation to contribute to the collective happiness by avoiding any cause for sadness or boredom, by appearing to be happy even if in the depths of despair."

Continual happiness is the unspoken mandate of our lives, but it is an unrealistic goal. No one is happy all of the time. Happiness is a fleeting emotion. It comes and goes. It is through the painful experiences of our lives that we grow, become more sensitive, empathetic and compassionate for others in similar situations and learn more about our own values and emotions.

Illness and death are not "happy" events, and because they contrast so sharply with our irrational pursuit of happiness, they are denied in ourselves and in others.

Mourning is thought to be morbid. People are uncomfortable around someone grieving. It is very difficult for people grieving today to find the necessary support to aid them in resolving their grief. It is risky to ask someone to listen to your weeping and wailing. Friends who don't know how to help you may reject you. In spite of these fears, I encourage you to reach out and ask for help when you want it. There are loving, caring people who will respond to your needs. If family and friends aren't the answer, another option is joining a self-help group where people in similar situations share their feelings, fears and frustrations. There are several around, and new ones are being formed all the time. Some are listed in Appendix B.

All across the country, there are services and programs for widows that provide information about insurance, financial investments, community resources, and emotional support. Another group, Parents of Murdered Children, was formed in 1978 in Cincinnati, and chapters are starting in other cities. Members say that they found a lack of support elsewhere, that they felt let down by families, friends, co-workers, members of their churches, and the criminal justice system. They come together twice a week and help each other deal with the anguish and pain of their grieving.

Another national group called Compassionate Friends has chapters in several countries. This group supports parents who have lost a child of any age.

These are only a few examples of such groups; there are others for survivors of suicide, for parents with terminally ill children, and so on. If you don't find an organization in your community to meet your needs, start one. It is much easier to share your grief than try to go it alone. You will help yourself and others at the same time.

Steps in Saying Goodbye

Mourning is not a disease. It is a normal and natural process that allows the separation to slowly become a reality. In those first few dreadful days, when you feel numb with shock and disbelief, the ritual of the funeral serves the purpose of keeping you busy, of bringing support from loved ones, and of giving you time to begin to come to terms with your loss.

The ceremony of the funeral makes accepting the reality of the death a little easier. The activity involved in notifying relatives and friends, choosing a funeral home, a casket, clothes, music, and the type of burial are all necessary and time-consuming. You may go through these preparations in a dream-like state, but the busyness keeps you involved in being practical, making decisions, and staying in touch with ongoing everyday responsibilities.

The ritual of the funeral provides a safe and supportive environment for those who had the closest connections with the dead person. It is a place to express their feelings and to receive support from others.

The funeral is the time to acknowledge and honor your loved one publicly, and to get support. A priest, rabbi, or minister generally delivers the eulogy. Members of the family and friends may speak. This is the final farewell to the physical body of the person you knew and loved; now only memories remain.

Some funeral directors understand the need for a more personal goodbye and will let families who request it be involved in the preparation of the body. Remember: burial rituals and funerals are for the living – a separation rite, a chance to come to terms with the reality of the death. An ending.

Memorial services with a closed casket and a favorite photograph of the deceased are becoming more popular. I recently attended a lovely memorial service for the mother of a good friend, in which special personal belongings were on hand, including her golf clubs and a hat she loved. Personal eulogies were written and read aloud by family members and friends. Others in attendance were invited to share their memories of the deceased. Her favorite music was played. One piece was the Christmas carol "Silent Night," even though the funeral was in the middle of the summer. An informal tea and a receiving line of relatives, which allowed those in attendance to express their condolences and offer support, followed the formal memorial service.

An artist friend who had been in precarious health planned for a party to be held at his home a few weeks after his death. Close friends were invited, and his favorite foods were served. Photos of his work and art projects were displayed. His personality seemed to be present. The event became a celebration of the creativity and beauty he had brought to the world as much as an occasion to mourn his loss.

In contrast, I went to a funeral where family members were segregated in a small room during the brief ceremony at the funeral parlor, then whisked off to the graveyard alone. As a result, they missed the opportunity to receive support from those who made the effort to come and be with them.

Children Need to Mourn Too

One of the worst things we can do is to prevent children from being involved in the death rituals of the funeral and burial in an attempt to protect them from the pain associated with death. In the past, when most children were raised on farms, death was a regular occurrence. Animals were slaughtered for food, or were sometimes attacked and killed by other animals, or baby animals died. Birth and death were taken in stride, not always without hurt, pain and grief, but as natural experiences. Children witnessed these events and learned to accept them as a normal part of life.

Today's child, raised in the city away from the natural reality of death, may be totally unprepared to cope with the death of a parent or a grandparent. Whenever children are exposed to death, every opportunity should be taken to talk frankly about what death means and how they feel about it. Ideally, the first time would be the funeral of a distant relative or acquaintance. Children should be encouraged to examine and talk about their feelings.

Open discussion about the possibility of the death of any family member should be an ongoing process. All questions should be answered sincerely and honestly. Options about disposal of the body should be discussed, such as donating organs for transplant, and preferences for burial or cremation. Children should be involved in plans about special music, flowers, or substitute donations to research organizations like the heart fund or cancer research, a children's home or a drug rehabilitation program.

Putting Affairs in Order

Financial matters should be worked out in advance to cover the death of one or both spouses. Plans should be made for the guardianship of minors. Children should be included in such family conversations as soon as they are able to understand the information. Wills should be made and reviewed regularly. A special file should be kept on insurance benefits, pension plans, Social Security, and investments. At least once a year this information should be discussed and reviewed, and the file should be revised when necessary.

Death may still be the last taboo in our country, but for grieving survivors, the chores of sorting through the chaos of business papers, money worries, estate taxes, and possibly having to sell the family home and move, can be the cruelest legacy you leave behind.

To put off taking care of these matters is to deny the reality of death. You cannot do the grieving for your loved ones, but you can spare them some of the anger and frustrations about money and financial survival that follow your death. This applies to both women and men, parents and adult children. Inform yourself about these matters now, while you can still do something about them.

Offering Comfort

Grieving doesn't end with the funeral. It has barely begun. Mourning is intensely personal. No two people grieve alike. During the weeks and months after a loss, some survivors will express deep emotions by crying; others will quietly reflect.

In offering support and comfort to a friend or relative who is grieving, it is important to avoid platitudes and trite sayings. Don't give advice or explanations. Death is a mystery. No one understands why death occurs, or the timing of death. Trying to explain only interferes with the pain of the bereaved, especially if the explanation sounds superficial and insincere.

The best way to offer support to friends is to let them know that you are there, perhaps hold their hands and listen. Listen actively. Don't relate your experiences. Be there with them, for them. Pitch in and help, don't wait to be asked. It is always appreciated when you bring food or drinks, or run errands. (See Appendix A)

It takes a lot of love and sensitivity to allow your friend to express grief in the way that is most helpful to him or her. Remember that the expression of grief is crucial to healing. Suppressing feelings will only lead to physical and emotional problems later. Talking about it is healing. Listen to their story.

Understanding Your Own Grief

When someone you love dies and you don't feel normal, you may wonder what is wrong with you. There is nothing wrong with you. Part of what is wrong is our current social attitude about death and dying.

Cultural influences are subtle, but powerful. Today people do not know what to expect while mourning. They wonder, what is normal? How long will it go on? Will I ever feel a joy for living again?

Yes, you will return to a "normal" life, a complete life of your own, in time. It won't happen the day after the funeral. The closer and more complex your relationship with the person who died, the more painful and involved and lengthy will be the process of letting go.

Saying goodbye takes time. It's helpful to understand the steps in the process, the conflicting emotions you may feel, and to know that you're working out your grief in the way that's necessary and unique to you. Be kind and gentle with yourself.

CHAPTER TWO

STAGES OF GRIEF

We are all different. Each person is an accumulation of genetic material, culture, family backgrounds, personal experiences, and unique coping styles. So when we experience the death of a loved and treasured person, we react in slightly different ways based on these factors. Each of us is unique, a composite of multiple influences.

Yet grieving follows a predictable pattern: while each of us goes through the steps in that pattern in our own way, it helps to know that others understand our feelings.

This book is written with the hope that when you or someone you know has lost a special person, you will have some idea of what to expect during the time of grief and mourning. And to let you know that in time you will recover and begin again to feel a joy in living.

A loss of someone in death is a wound, and as with any injury, illness, or physical wound, you must give yourself time to heal. The psychological pain that you will feel is just as important as any observable physical wound. Time gives you distance from the events of the death and the personal relationship that you had with that person. Time alone will not heal you, but the timing of the grieving process will help you to become whole again if you allow yourself to experience and feel what you must to release the deceased and to get on with your own life.

Traditionally, the official time of mourning has been one year. This is common in many cultures and religions. Judaism, for example, organizes the mourning year into four sections – three days of deep grief, seven days of mourning, thirty days of gradual adjustment, and eleven months of readjustment for remembrance and healing.

Often, one year is not enough time. In the loss of a spouse or child, for instance, two years or more may be a more realistic expectation of the time needed to heal and recover. If the grieving process is allowed to run its natural course, there is a typical time frame that you can anticipate.

The steps are as follows:

Stage I -   Breaking Old Habits
             Time of death to eight weeks

Stage II -   Beginnings of Reconstruction of Life
             Eight weeks to one year

Stage III - Seeking New Love Objects or Friends
             One year to two years

Stage 1V -   Readjustment Complete
             After two years

The Grieving Process

These times are not rigid; rather, persons who have gone through a grieving process generally report a flexible guideline of what they experienced. Much depends, of course, on the degree of intimacy you have had with the person who died. If it was a spouse or child with whom you were living, then it will be a more profound experience than if you didn't live with the person. For instance, if you lose someone you did not live with, he or she may be on your mind a lot, but you will not be in the habit of expecting him or her to come home to supper. You won't have that daily reminder of absence.

Another important factor is your prior knowledge of the coming loss. If there was a long, serious illness and you had a chance to begin your grieving before the death, you may move through the stages of grief faster.

Let's examine in more detail these stages of present and future adjustments, which are necessary to move through grief to a renewed life.

Stage I: Breaking Old Habits (Death to eight weeks)

The weeks immediately following a death are a time of numbness and confusion. Nothing is normal. Feelings of shock, disbelief, protest, and denial are rampant. Death is a forced separation; a tearing apart. You feel severed and raw, your emotions scattered to the wind. If the death was sudden and unexpected, the anguish is more acute. You may feel an actual physical shock when you first get the news.

Your life is changed from the instant you are told about

the death. You feel helpless and powerless to control the events of your life. At the same time you are swept along in a rapid tide of activity. Daily responsibilities continue and you must go on and meet them. Decisions must be made. Notifying relatives and friends, funeral arrangements, newspaper notices, death certificates, and a myriad of other details demand your attention.

Often the activity is a blessing in disguise. You are involved in the final act of giving or paying tribute to your loved one. The busyness helps you through the first few days, giving you a chance to begin to realize the reality of your loss. But you are extremely vulnerable now and need to protect yourself at all levels.

Habits and Patterns

As the confusion clears a little, you begin to be more aware of the need to adjust to letting go of the habit patterns in the relationship. When people live together, lots of habits are formed. Small ways of interacting are often taken for granted. Things such as expecting your spouse to bring the newspaper into the house, telephoning your mate at a certain time each day, seeing the towels left on the bathroom floor, sleeping on one side of the bed, sitting at a certain place at meals – these are second nature. When these routine situations are interrupted, you must reprogram your expectations at the emotional, physical, and psychic levels. Daily, there are little reminders that the fabric of your life has been torn. You will feel deep sadness, deprivation, and loss.

Leslie, a teacher, had a habit of making mental notes of events on her job each day to tell her husband about in the evening. After his death, she would catch herself thinking of telling him about something and realize with a start that such sharing would not happen. At first the tears came in torrents with the realization that he wouldn't be there. Her feelings of self-pity, loneliness, and helplessness were overwhelming. But gradually, slowly, she came to realize that he was gone and to accept his death and stop anticipating their old behavior patterns. Now, eight months later, she hardly ever thinks of him in that context. She shares her stories with other teachers or occasionally with friends.

As the reality of the loss is accepted, the futility of anticipating former routine events is realized, and in time, changes in lifestyle are recognized and eventually appreciated. Gradually, loneliness changes to enjoying time alone to think or to be creative, to begin or finish projects long waiting for attention.

Some people eat more when they are feeling deprived as a way to nurture themselves. Other people eat less, lose their appetites completely and stop cooking meals. Food loses taste for most people. These disturbances last only a short time and clear up naturally. If they persist for many weeks, you may want to make an effort to change them, or to seek counseling to talk about your progress or where you are stuck.

During this early time, a grieving person may experience changes in everyday living, such as eating and sleeping habits. Sleep is often restless and may include disturbing dreams, waking in the middle of the night and not being able to go back to sleep, or waking at 5:00 A.M. exhausted and tense.

The Deceased's Presence

Tears and feelings of profound sadness come up at unexpected times. You may be watching a movie or television program, driving a car, shopping for groceries, sitting in church, or playing tennis; any time that thoughts of the dead person arise is a potential time for tears. It is very important to let those feelings of sadness out. It is cleansing, purifying, if you allow yourself to experience the tears, and you will recover more quickly. Stopping yourself from crying serves no function, and letting the tears flow will bring some release of pain.

In the early weeks of grieving it is common and normal to be preoccupied – even obsessed – with the dead person. In fact, you may feel disloyal if you do not have her on your mind constantly.

Talking to your deceased child or spouse or parent is one way to release stress. Going to the grave, writing letters to him, keeping a journal, or having an imaginary conversation are all ways to complete the unfinished business in the relationship. It is irrelevant whether the deceased hears the messages or not; like funerals, this is for you.

There are always things left unsaid, business left unfinished, when someone dies. By continuing to communicate to your dead loved one, you can complete the relationship. Many people report a sensing or feeling of the presence of the deceased around them. These experiences are neither strange nor abnormal; they can be a great comfort to the survivor and in time will begin to seem less important.

Marty recently told me that he knew his dead wife was

"around" and that if she could talk, she would give him hell for buying a new car. After making joint decisions for years, it is only natural that he would know how his former mate would respond to his choices. Marty continued to consider her probable reactions as he shopped for a car, even though she had been dead for almost a year. In his thoughts, he had conversations with her to satisfy himself.

Marty's "talks" with his late wife were a way of continuing to include her in his life, acknowledging her importance to him. Old patterns take time to break. Part of keeping her "alive" in his mind means still consulting her.

But by the time Marty buys his next car, her input will be less important to him.

Go Easy on Yourself

Children, pets, aging parents, job stresses and any other demands must be put in the background as much as possible during this early grieving period. Mental confusion and low energy levels are very common. Fatigue and exhaustion result both from expending energy to cope and resisting the emotional responses that continue to surface. This is not a good time to make any major decisions.

The simplest habits of daily living, such as shopping, eating, sleeping or dressing may become burdensome for a while. But every day you survive takes you farther along the path to recovery.

Stage II: Beginning to Reconstruct Your Life
          (Eight weeks to one year)

Even after a few months have passed, your pain and

confusion are still acute. But they gradually diminish, and recovery begins to take place automatically and without conscious awareness. You are healing. Habit patterns will still be erratic and in a state of flux, changing from the former established routines.

Sally's husband loved romaine lettuce. She didn't like it, but automatically continued to buy it when she shopped for groceries. She would take it home, wash it and store it in the refrigerator until it spoiled and she had to throw it out. After three months, it finally dawned on her that she didn't have to buy romaine lettuce anymore. Small changes like this reduce the denial of death and let reality slowly creep in.

If you are stuck, go get some help, whether it takes one visit or several until you feel better able to cope on your own.

Overall health may be of concern. You may be physically run down and more vulnerable and susceptible to minor illnesses like viruses, sinusitis or flues. Major sickness can easily occur now, especially illnesses that are directly stress-related, such as colitis or digestive tract disorders like gastritis and ulcers. Blood pressure changes can occur; even heart diseases or cancer may show up.

Accidents are more likely to happen during periods of extreme stress. We are all more prone to accidents when suffering from emotional stress and unresolved feelings. Take extra precautions when driving, hiking, or engaging in other activities.

It is very important to be as gentle to yourself as possible and to avoid adding any more stressful situations to your life for a while. Try to eat well, get the best sleep that you can, take naps, exercise regularly, and allow yourself to feel and experience any emotions that may arise. Cry when you need to. Seeds for chronic illnesses can be planted under the tension of the grieving process and may pop out several years later if your emotions are denied or repressed.

Emotional disturbances continue to require a great deal of energy for the first year. Spontaneous crying at unexpected times and places can be surprising and sometimes embarrassing. Seeing a happy family or watching a romantic scene on television or at a movie often strike a sentimental nerve and rekindle feelings of loss and deprivation. Tears flow and wash away more of the pain. It's okay – in fact, it's mentally healthy and normal – to feel sad and cry. It's cleansing, healing.

Worry and feelings of helplessness are common early in the grieving process and are normal aspects of the depression experienced in grief. Concern about being able to take care of yourself, of meeting basic survival needs, of having the energy to get through another day, may surface from time to time. Thinking that the present feelings may never end contributes to self-pity and helplessness. These feelings are normal and in time will pass.

Memory lapses are also common now. Marge told me that she misplaced the settlement check from her late husband's life insurance policy. It was missing for weeks, as she searched everywhere. She felt stupid to have lost something so important to her survival. Finally, she looked through a box of scrap papers that she was about to throw away and she found the check, which she had unconsciously thrown out. Another subconscious form of denial? Probably. And, given her state of mental confusion, understandable carelessness.

Thoughts of suicide may surface from time to time. These are normal and common. If, however, they become obsessive and linger in your mind, get some professional help. Being dead yourself may look like an easy way out of your misery. It isn't. It's a cop-out. Everyone who loves you and depends on you would be left with the double whammy of dealing with two deaths.

Suicide during grief is the ultimate in self-pity and helplessness, not a solution to anything. So when such thoughts come up, notice them and let them pass. There's no need to dwell on them or wallow in them or worry about them. Let them go and get on with your life. Your life is necessary and important and unique and valuable. You are the survivor, not a victim. Don't get stuck in the victim mode.

Dwelling on the circumstances of the death and negative parts of the relationship will only delay your recovery time. You may think frequently about your unresolved conflicts, feel guilt about mistakes or the things you didn't do, and now wish you had. Whatever happened between you, you did the best you could at the time. Continually going over situations cannot change them. Forgive yourself if there is anything to forgive that is still unfinished. Forgive your spouse or parent or child for anything left unresolved or unsaid. Begin to think in positive terms of the good times in the relationship, and give up the painful ones. Above all, stop punishing yourself.

Much of the healing process is unconscious. Dreams, daydreams, and fantasies are clues to how you are doing as you progress through the first year. Dreaming of the dead person is part of processing and letting go. A dream log can be very helpful and valuable if you need to seek counseling at some time. You can keep track of the progression of your dreams by writing about each one in a notebook. Record them as soon as you wake up. If you have trouble remembering your dreams at first, just suggest to yourself as you begin to fall asleep that you want to remember your dreams, and you will soon begin to remember them. Record as much detail as possible; include the setting, time of the day or night, colors, people, how you feel, vehicles, water, animals, and other details. Dreams recorded over a period of time reveal more information than a single dream.

Betsy had a series of dreams about water. Water for her was symbolic of the flow of her life. In her early dreams, shortly after her husband's death, she was in a boat that was about to turn over, and she was struggling not to fall into the water, which was cold and frightening. Later dreams revealed the water to be less deep, but still cold and dark. Gradually, over a year, the water in her dreams became warmer and clearer, and in the last recorded water dream, she was playing and swimming in it. She was ready to get back in the swim of life!

Special Times

Holidays and family celebrations will be very hard the first year. Birthdays, Christmas, and other sentimental holidays are the worst ones without the one you've lost. But it gets easier each time. Try to have those you love best and who are most supportive around you for these occasions. You may feel prepared to "get through" these times and try to steel yourself against the inevitable hurt. You're not steel – you are human. Even though these special days will be hard and painful, you can stand it. In fact, you will feel surprisingly relieved afterwards. The second time will be easier.

Allow yourself to feel sadness, disappointment, resentment, anger, or any other emotion that comes up. To feel nothing – just a kind of numbness – is okay as long as it's not a way of blocking emotions. You will experience your emotions when you are ready to. I encourage you not to block the emotions when they surface. Experience them, feel them, and then put them behind you.

Sheila, a young widow, thought she was all ready for her first holiday season after her husband's death. At a big family Thanksgiving dinner, she wouldn't allow herself to feel sad. She was pleased that it was so easy. She had worried that she would have feelings of sadness and pain, and made every effort to enjoy herself and not feel depressed. Three days later, she went to visit relatives in another city. Sheila spent the entire visit sick in bed, with severe pains in her stomach and back. This physical breakdown was her way of coping with the emotional pain that she repressed on Thanksgiving Day. Instead of letting the feelings out, she fought them, turned them inward, and later got sick.

Next year it should be much easier for Sheila. By the second year, new family rituals will begin to be established, and her dead husband will be missed less.

Another difficult date is the anniversary of the death. This is especially hard if the death occurred around a holiday or someone's birthday. Remember, each year it gets easier to handle. You will survive! You will grow with new areas of strength and courage in your life that you never realized you had. Make a conscious choice toward life and accept the pain that is part of it.

Rediscovering Yourself

Searching for and establishing a new and separate personal identity is a major part of this second stage of recovery. It is a slow process that can be both painful and joyous. You may still feel married, or still feel you have a best friend, even though she's gone. If your child has died, you may feel that your life has no meaning. You miss him terribly!

Some people, in coping with a major loss, immerse themselves in a flurry of activity. Many get wholeheartedly involved in outside activities, in work, finding a new job, or returning to school. There can be a "driven" aspect to this – a compulsion to "throw" yourself into something and always be busy so you won't have to think about or feel the pain. This is another form of the denial process, a way to avoid the work of grieving.

If you feel that your relationship somehow involved personal failure on your part, then it seems all the more important to prove your worth, especially to yourself. Staying busy is a way to try to fill your mind with other information, pressures, and demands so that you will not have to think about your lost loved one or your emotional state. You hope that involvement in external events will make the internal pain disappear. Unfortunately, it doesn't work! You will have to complete your grieving process or eventually suffer the consequences. Face the guilt feelings so you can put them behind you for good. Forgive yourself and let it go.

If you're not using activity to dull your emotions, begin to search for your special skills, interests and ways to grow and to support yourself. Many people have found returning to school both rewarding and a good way to make new friends, especially for widows. Begin to set positive goals for yourself.

Vocational or job training is another option. One young widow I know enrolled in a special school to become a travel agent. She plans to use her insurance settlement to buy or start her own travel agency.

Moving to another home or city may be tempting during this first year. It is better to avoid doing this if possible. Most often such moves are impulsive and later regretted.

By the anniversary of the death, you will be aware that you are somewhat better and renewed. You have a way to go, but you have accepted your loss and are beginning to plan your future.

Stage III: Seeking New Love Objects or Friends (12 months to 24 months)

Life has returned to "normal." Some former habits are firmly re-established and new habits have become routine. Daily tasks are automatic. Emotional pain is less acute.

Your loved one is not in your thoughts as often.

Mourning may continue as a ritual, but the intensity has greatly diminished and will not be as devastating as earlier. You will seldom cry in public, although there will still be moments of sadness and depression. Depression is an outer manifestation of an internal struggle. The internal struggle throughout the entire mourning process is to come to terms with the reality of your loss and to find a new identity and rebuild your life.

Renewed Health

After the first year, eating and sleeping habits should have returned to normal. Laughter, fun, happiness, and a sense of humor are returning. Smoking and use of alcohol and drugs return to the pre-loss patterns in the second year. Memory is normal. You are making new future plans, maybe for a trip or a class.

Health usually returns to normal or may be better than before, provided that the emotional issues and pain of the bereavement have been dealt with and released.

You'll experience heavy emotional reactions less and less often. Anger, resentment, guilt, anxiety, and fears of being able to survive on your own should be part of the past now, or rapidly fading away. Dreams will have lighter content and portray a mood of involvement in life.

Friends

You will have made new friends, some of whom will have had similar experiences. Start planning interesting leisure time activities with new people or dear old friends. Maybe a trip, a new recreational activity, political action, volunteer work, classes, learning a language, whatever you want to do. Get involved.

If you are working, you will be better at managing your time and responsibilities. All members of the family will begin to come to terms with your new relationships and changes in the family after adjusting to the absence of the dead person.

One day you will wake up and know that the healing process has been working. You realize that your thinking is sharper and clearer, that your judgment and perceptions are more rational and reliable, that your emotions have settled down and you are less preoccupied with yourself. Overall, you feel more alive and happy. You made it!

Stage IV: Readjustment Completed (After the second year)

This final stage is characterized by the end of mourning. Routine habits of life have blended, old patterns and new patterns come together and are carried out without conscious thought. You are living your new life.

Living space, working arrangements, childcare, leisure time activities, dating and other friendships and relationships have pretty well settled into a comfortable flow. Life is less fragmented and hectic. You will be less "self" occupied and more "other" occupied. You have a new life and a new philosophy.

There will be times of euphoria and contentment. The future will seem bright. You will feel stronger than ever, and you will know now that you can survive any loss. You may not want to, but you know that you can. Now you know that pain passes in time, and the growth you achieve can be personally very rewarding.

Overall, your new life has become normal for you. You feel that you are a different person, and in many ways you are. If you have used the time of mourning to slowly heal and have allowed yourself to experience and express the deep and often painful emotions that have been brought to the surface in your grieving, you will now be ready for the next chapter of your life. Welcome it and enjoy the strength you now have to face new challenges that await you. Welcome back to the world of the living and the loving.

One way to test your recovery is to check how much of the time your loved one is now on your mind. At first you are engulfed in thinking about him or her 100% of the time. By the end of the second year, the percentage drops to 10% or less. This is fine. You are moving on with your own life.

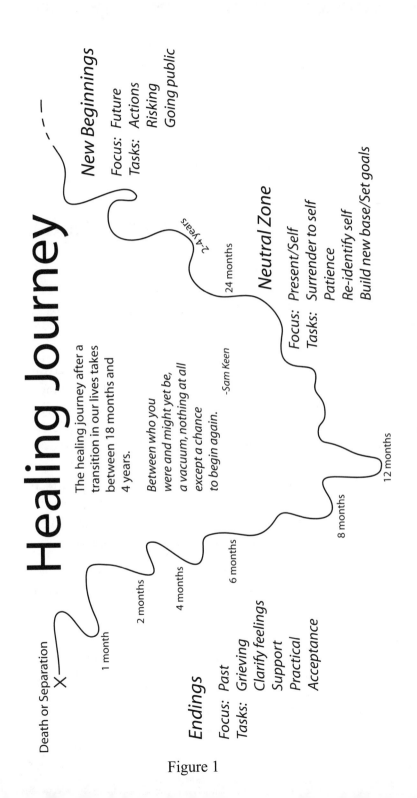

Healing Journey

Death or Separation
X

The healing journey after a transition in our lives takes between 18 months and 4 years.

Between who you were and might yet be, a vacuum, nothing at all except a chance to begin again.

—Sam Keen

1 month
2 months
4 months
6 months
8 months
12 months
24 months
2-4 years

Endings

Focus: Past
Tasks: Grieving
Clarify feelings
Support
Practical
Acceptance

Neutral Zone

Focus: Present/Self
Tasks: Surrender to self
Patience
Re-identify self
Build new base/Set goals

New Beginnings

Focus: Future
Tasks: Actions
Risking
Going public

Figure 1

CHAPTER THREE

FEELINGS OF GRIEF

The feelings of grief last far longer than society in general realizes or allows. Even closest friends may expect us to be back to "normal" in a few weeks after a death. But living with loss is not so simple. The death of someone close may cause emotional pain and confusion for months or even years. Losing someone we love through death is one of the most traumatic of life's experiences. Acute grief affects several million people every year. And it occurs to every one of us at some time in our lives. Several times, if we live a long life. People we love die and we mourn their loss.

Almost two million people die every year in the United States – and nearly every one of them leaves behind someone who mourns their loss.

Other changes cause grief: there are over one million divorces per year; thousands more people separate from spouses. Children, relatives, and friends suffer from the turmoil and confusion of losing a valuable relationship.

Separation is the critical event, be it by death, divorce or abandonment.

People leave careers, have accidents, and grow older. All significant life changes involve a grieving process as we say goodbye to part of the old self, old ways, and familiar paths. We must adjust to the new ones.

Being able to manage grief is important for both the individual experiencing a loss, and for the society of which he or she is part. Management of grief means handling it: understanding your feelings, living with the loss and change, fitting the events of a death or change and its aftermath into your life, so that *you* can go on living.

The stresses of unsuccessful, uncompleted grieving can lead to serious physical illness, lost hours from a job, mental distress, and even death.

As traumatic and difficult as it can be, loss is not rare. It is universal. No one in the world escapes some time in life when he or she must come to terms with a loss through death, illness, separation or other dramatic change. The process of grieving is also universal, and it is subject to cultural influences such as the rituals of death and burial. The prevailing social attitudes dictate how emotions are expressed.

Dr. Elisabeth Kubler-Ross, a psychiatrist who worked with patients who had terminal illnesses, has broken down the grief process into five identifiable stages. She discovered that most patients experienced periods of denial, anger, bargaining, and depression before reaching acceptance. These feelings, usually appearing in the order that Kubler-

Ross identified, are common to all of us when we are faced with adjusting to changes in our lives, both positive and negative changes.

Thanks to the pioneering work of Dr. Kubler-Ross, we can help people know what to expect when tragedy strikes. However, we are all unique personalities. Not everyone moves through these stages in the same way or with the same timing. Some people get stuck in one stage or another and never move on to the final stage of acceptance and of rebuilding their lives. Others experience the feelings more than once, perhaps reaching depression, then going back to denial or anger.

Let's look at the five stages.

Denial

The shock of finding out that someone died is felt by some people as a physical jolt. A state of numbness and disbelief takes hold. This is a protective state, which insulates the bereaved from the anguish that will follow in the coming months in coming to terms with the death. The denial stage usually lasts from four to six weeks. Sometimes a person feels guilty during this time because she doesn't "feel" anything. She may not cry at the funeral, or she may take care of others who are expressing their grief. This is normal. You do not need to force yourself to feel something that is not natural for you, but don't hold back your feelings either when they start to surface. After about six weeks, if a person is stoically fighting his grief and strong feelings, or is still feeling numb, he is denying his feelings and is headed for emotional trouble.

The benefit of the time of denial is to mobilize your inner resources to allow you to face the reality of your new situation. As you collect yourself, it is time to begin looking at what has happened and to acknowledge other feelings.

Anger

Anger may be expressed outwardly as rage, or turned inward and be experienced as depression. But underneath all anger is fear. Fear of meeting your own needs, of making decisions, fear that you won't be able to manage financial, emotional, and physical survival.

When anger is expressed outwardly, a person may project it onto other people. She may be angry with the doctor for not giving adequate care, or at the policeman who was insensitive when he told her of the death. He may be furious at his mother for telling him what to do with the children during the funeral. They may be angry with God, for the injustice and unfairness of the death. Blaming others is a way of avoiding the personal pain and sorrow and despair of coming to terms with the fact that your life goes on without the dead person.

The danger for a person who projects her anger onto others is that she may become caught up in bitterness, resentment, and alienation. As young children, we are taught by well-meaning parents that to express anger is wrong, is not nice, is unbecoming, so we learn to stuff our feelings inside. We learn to deny any feelings *like* anger, such as irritation, resentment, frustration, disappointment, terror, fear, or hurt. We love and need our parents; we want their approval, so we do as we are told and we deny and hide our feelings.

Unfortunately, we must learn to reverse this process later in our lives. The death of a loved one is a time of emotional testing. Our emotions are part of us, and by acknowledging and owning them we can reach new levels of sensitivity, love, and self-awareness.

First, admit your anger. You'll find that you aren't simply angry with the doctor – you may also be angry at the husband or parent who died and left you. Many people tell me, "How can I be angry at my child? She didn't want to die." Of course not, but you may feel angry at losing her, at the strong feelings you now feel, at the financial aspects. There may not be a real target for your anger; sometimes life is unfair. We all have different reasons for feeling what we feel. Your feelings are legitimately part of you; don't be ashamed of them. Hiding your anger won't make it disappear. You'll get past it more quickly if you bring it out into the open.

After you admit your anger to yourself, talk about it with someone you trust. This may be frightening to you, but anger accumulates and will erupt eventually, maybe frightening or hurting another person. A good friend or a professional counselor will help you work through your feelings of anger or fear. Learning to recognize and deal with milder emotions when they arise is the best way to avoid the explosive out-of-control outbursts of anger turned to rage.

Begin to notice when you feel irritated, hurt or disappointed. As you start to handle these emotions at the time they occur, you will notice that your anger is more easily controlled.

When anger does build up to the point of explosion, there

are techniques that you can use to let off the steam without hurting yourself or other people. Because pent-up emotions are stored in the body, one way to release them is through physical activity. Screaming or beating on a pillow or tearing up a telephone book can be helpful. Take a long walk, chop wood, or work out in a gym. Go swimming or take up a physical activity you enjoyed in the past. Get involved with such an activity on a regular basis for a while. Concentrate on your body, not your grief.

If you scream or beat on a pillow, you will get some immediate and temporary relief. Find a private place alone and shout or talk out your present frustrations. This is helpful, but only a temporary solution to let off steam. Plan a longer-term program to continue to get into contact with your feelings and handle them. Getting counseling, and/or joining a group with other people who have had a similar death in their family, is an excellent idea. If you have a problem with old unresolved issues, join an anger management group.

Finally, turn the energy of your anger into doing something positive. Start a self-help group for others who had a similar death in their families: for instance, begin a program to train ambulance drivers or police officers to be more sensitive to the dying. One woman whose daughter was killed by a car driven by a drunken driver started MADD (Mothers Against Drunk Driving). The organization has spread all over the country and influenced legislation to curb driving while intoxicated. (See Appendix B.)

Bargaining

Bargaining before the death occurs may include wishing

that a new miraculous cure will be found, or wanting to live until after your next birthday or Christmas or Hanukkah, or making deals with God that the disease is misdiagnosed. Bargaining goes on in our minds to help buy time to accept the truth of the situation.

After the death, bargaining is less important. You soon realize that fantasies of trying to bring the person back to life are unrealistic. They only delay the necessary responsibility to emotionally release the loved one who died. Eventually, as you begin to make new friends and get involved in new activities, you will live less in the past, and your dreams of how it could have been will fade.

Depression

Depression is often defined as anger turned inward. It includes feelings of helplessness, hopelessness, and powerlessness. Depression is a mood disturbance. It includes feelings of sadness, disappointment, and loneliness. When a person is depressed, he often withdraws from people and activities, loses capacity for pleasure and avoids the enjoyable activities formerly experienced in life. You may notice physical discomforts such as aches, pains, fatigue, poor digestion, and sleep disturbances. Moderate depression is normal after someone dies. For a while, you may want to be alone to sort out your feelings and to begin to make plans for the future.

If your symptoms are severe and lasting, so that you completely lose interest in the outside world, then get professional help. You may find that one day you feel pretty good and the next day you awake with a sense of doom and gloom. This is okay for a while; in time, the days of feeling good will outnumber the bad days.

To help yourself during this time, take care of the things that need your attention. Don't put off handling financial and other matters, or they will accumulate and overwhelm you later. Ask for comfort and help when you want it. Try to do something special for yourself each day, something that you really like. Take a hot bubble bath, treat yourself to an ice cream cone, listen to music, read for an hour, talk a walk or a nap, or whatever is enjoyable to you. Exercise and a good diet will also relieve some of your depression.

Some people get stuck in depression. It is important to neither resist your feelings nor wallow in them. Do something physically active which will help you to sleep better. While you are walking, running, swimming, or playing tennis, concentrate on your body, not on your sadness. Listening to *relaxing* soothing environmental sounds or music is very helpful in reducing your stress and depression.

Guilt

Guilt comes from something we did or said that we wish that we had not done; or from something that we think that we should have said or done that we didn't do. Whenever you find yourself saying *should* or *ought*, you are putting yourself in a position to feel guilt. You may have legitimately and purposely avoided, neglected, injured or damaged another person. If so, then you must take responsibility for your behavior and make amends as well as you can.

On the other hand, you may be creating unreasonable guilt for yourself. If you are saying to yourself or others,

"He wouldn't have had the accident if only I hadn't bought him that car," you are creating your guilt by your self-talk. *If only* and *What if* are questions that can never be answered. You do not have the facts available to know what else could have happened. You must rid yourself of the irrational *if only* things you are saying to yourself. These thoughts serve no purpose but to keep you feeling guilty, and guilt delays your healing.

Feeling guilt will slow down your recovery. Even if you're convinced that your actions were wrong or insensitive, you must forgive yourself and go on with your life. If you were a jerk, then learn a lesson from the experience and don't repeat it. Feeling guilty over a prolonged time is a choice you are making. You can also choose not to feel guilty. You must accept the reality of what has happened. The death or separation cannot be changed now, but you can change what you think about it. You don't need to become a martyr. No human is perfect – only perfectly human, and that includes making mistakes. Mistakes become valuable when we learn from them. What have you learned from yours?

Interrelationship of Body, Mind and Emotions

Human beings function in life on different levels: the mind or intellect, the emotional or feeling level, and the physical level. The intellectual, reasoning, analytical part is a function of the left hemisphere of our brains. The emotional, feeling, creative part is governed more by the right side of our brains. Our limbic brain, a part of our nervous system, regulates our primitive, emotional response to danger and fearful experiences. When we perceive danger, we react with a fight-or-flight survival response, just as animals do.

At the physical level, our bodies gather information constantly through our five senses, reporting this information about stress level, body temperature, pain, danger and illness through our nervous system to our brains. We process information as thoughts. Our thoughts in turn influence our emotions. All three systems are interrelated, and all are necessary to survival. They work together to form a whole balanced system. Holistic health is a philosophy that teaches people to tune into these integral parts of us and to strive to maintain balance.

When one part is ignored, we become out of balance. For example, if you ignore the body's signals to the brain – by constant overeating, continuing to smoke when you have a chronic lung disease, or not sleeping when you are exhausted – in time your body will break down. You will become ill and eventually die, perhaps prematurely.

Similarly, a person who ignores or denies strong and painful emotions will eventually break down emotionally, by having anxiety attacks, irrational outbursts of anger, or other neurotic or psychotic symptoms.

This imbalance also happens when a person tries to deal with emotions on an intellectual level, by rationalizing. It doesn't work. Thoughts are thoughts; they cannot be felt. Feelings are feelings; they cannot be thought.

Thoughts, however, affect feelings and the degree of the feelings can be regulated or stimulated by thoughts. This doesn't mean controlling your emotions by repressing and rationalizing them. It means not letting your negative emotions continue to make you feel bad after such feelings become unproductive. For example, if you use strong words in your thoughts like *terrible, never again, can't,* or *hate,* then your emotional reactions will be equally strong and may seem overwhelming to resolve. But if you use words like *I choose, may, examine, forgive, decide,* then you are making selections and are in control of your emotional choices.

Your thoughts are your self-talk: what goes on inside of your head. You may tune into this talk to take charge of what you're telling yourself. Your self-talk creates your reality. You can use your self-talk to set up emotional barriers, and feel completely helpless and emotionally impotent. Or you can expand your horizons and create positive change and growth. You are in charge and you, and you alone, create your own reality and your own life.

Acceptance

How will you know when you are well? When you can think of your loved one without strong emotional feelings of longing and sadness. You will remember him or her realistically, neither as an idealized saint nor as a villain. You will be living in the present, not stuck in the past, and you will be making plans for the future. You will be able to live with the ambiguity of the never-to-be-answered questions.

You will notice that he or she is in your thoughts less and less as you build your continuing life. You will be able to experience the joys and pleasures that life holds for all of us, alone or with others.

Growing, Renewal

The psychologist Carl Jung said that part of being human involves having problems, because human beings have a consciousness, as opposed to lower animals that operate their lives on instincts. Problems force us to a more developed consciousness, a fuller awareness of events and feelings. As Jung says, "Every one of us gladly turns away from his problems; if possible they must not be mentioned, or better still, their experience is denied. We wish to make our lives simple, certain and smooth. And for that reason problems are taboo. The artful denial of a problem will not produce conviction; on the contrary, a wider and higher consciousness is called for to give us the certainty and clarity we need."

For each death, each survivor feels a different set of reactions, and must work through the grieving processes at whatever pace and time is necessary for him or her. There are similarities among those who manage their grief successfully – and similar blocking patterns for those who have trouble resolving their grief. Focus on your patterns of grieving; monitor your self-talk and emotions to help you raise your consciousness and grow into a stronger, more sensitive person.

CHAPTER FOUR

DEATH OF A SPOUSE

The death of a spouse is a major psychological blow, one of life's biggest losses. Adjusting to and eventually accepting the reality of the death is a long, slow, and painful healing process. We are not prepared to experience the emotional devastation that the death of a husband or wife brings to us. It takes time to heal the psychological and emotional wound of being widowed. Slowly, little by little, you will heal. You can even grow from your grief. In time, you may become more sensitive to the suffering of others; you may find new areas of inner strength and talents within yourself.

When a spouse dies, all the sharing of dreams, the emotional closeness, the years of growth together will now become memories. In a marriage of many years, the two of you have been one in many functional and emotional ways. Now you are without that other half, and you may feel incomplete.

The loss of someone as fundamentally intimate and

important as your wife or husband will hurt deeply, and it will hurt for a long time, but not forever. In time you will get over the painful emotions of your loss. When your spouse dies, there is no hope of reconciliation. Death is irreversible. Death is final – and to accept this reality is one of the most difficult and painful adjustments you will make in your lifetime.

The word *widow* means empty, without a mate. Many cultures have traditional rituals and customs associated with widowhood, rituals that recognize the tragedy of losing a mate in death. But in the United States we have fewer specific norms or cultural guidelines for going through the stages of grief. In fact, we often seem to try to hide widowed persons away. Much of our society is couple-oriented, and couples don't know how a widow or widower fits in. Widows and widowers remind others of the fragile thread of their own relationships. So in a short time the grieving spouse is dropped from social lists and becomes invisible to former friends and associates.

Death is part of life, just as love is. Losing a mate may be the price we pay for love. We always take a risk when we involve ourselves in a relationship, because losing the loved one will be a trauma. The more intense the love and involvement, the greater the loss.

Your pain in bereavement is unique to you. Your relationship is unique to you. The circumstances of the death are special and unique to you. I will not presume to tell you how or when you will experience your grief. What I can do is to give you broad guidelines that may be helpful.

The Time Frame

If you knew that your spouse had a terminal illness and would die at some time in the near future, you may have begun to prepare yourself psychologically for the death. However, not everyone is realistic about facing such a reality. Some people continue to carry false hope in their hearts until the very end. Their resistance may add to their pain. Knowing ahead of time is like a gift, if that time is used to begin the grieving process, to begin to anticipate what life will be like without your mate.

You may even have had some mixed feelings before your spouse died. Watching a loved one suffer and feeling so helpless after all medical strategies have failed are extremely emotionally draining experiences. You may have wished that the end would hurry to relieve the suffering, yet at the same time felt guilty at having such thoughts, or anxious and fearful at losing your spouse. You may even have felt angry at the extra emotional and physical demands put upon you. Confused and conflicting feelings are normal at such a difficult time.

No matter how you used your warning time before the death, you will experience shock and disbelief when the death finally happens. The benefits of advance knowledge come later in the grieving process, when you begin to pick up the threads of your life. The extended time of grieving could be shorter and less severe if you began to grieve before the actual death.

If you had no prior warning and the death was unexpected, the initial period of shock and disbelief usually lasts longer.

There are more pieces of the relationship left hanging and incomplete. It takes longer to sort out your thoughts and feelings.

You will be in an acute grief reaction from the time of the death until about the end of one year. Your healing will be a slow and gradual process: small, progressive steps to begin to know that you will survive on your own. Some of the wounds of the past must heal before you can move into the future.

The second year is a time when you will begin to form new friendships, make changes, set goals and formulate plans involving your future. You will be more emotionally able to let go of the past and begin to look forward to the future.

Protect Yourself

During the first months, try to avoid making major demands on yourself; don't try to sort out all your feelings or plan your future. Take one day at a time. Moving, changing jobs and promotions are all stressful enough anyway. Adding any of these to the natural tension of early grief can bring about a dangerous overload on your psyche. So it's best not to make major changes in your work or residence during the first several months of widowhood.

During the first few weeks, a lot of time and energy will be required to handle practical matters following the funeral, such as death certificate, autopsy, coroner's reports, insurance company dealings, social security, bank accounts, charge accounts, probate court, selecting a headstone and similar business matters.

Other problems connected with everyday living may arise, such as getting the car serviced and repaired, keeping appliances running, getting the lawn cut, changing the name of the responsible party on utility bills, and doing the income tax. They may all sound insignificant, but such chores can seem overwhelming during this period of grieving. These activities help you get on with your own life, but if the tasks seem too difficult, ask for help from other members of the family, friends, or hire someone to take care of some of the demands.

Satisfaction with your life will be at a low point for a while. This is a time to coast. It's not a time to set goals, make any major decisions, or exercise choices that will have long-range effects. It is a time when you may feel a lot of confusion and a little craziness. Let the feelings happen. They will pass.

The confusion you feel is part of the natural healing process. Resistance will only prolong problems, so just let the reactions flow and soon you will evolve into the next stage of recovery. Be patient: progress in your healing is gradual, but you *are* moving. You are getting ready to rebuild your life.

During this early part of your recovery, you are adjusting to a state of acute emotional deprivation. This is a time to conserve your energy, reduce your frustrations, be patient and gentle with yourself. The pain of your loss will be felt in many large and small ways. Many widowed people report that they continue to sleep on "their" side of the bed and often reach out in sleep for the body of their spouse. Sometimes they awaken to realize with profound sadness the reality of the death. You will probably feel occasional twinges of depression and wishing that things could be the way they were before; gradually these times will pass.

Others in Your Life

Caring for younger children may be a burden during this first year. You may be too exhausted to get up and dress them for school or to make their breakfast. Sometimes you may be short-tempered and impatient. The kids may seem more difficult and more demanding than ever before. They may start acting up at school and at home, trying to get your attention and reassurance that you love them and that you will not leave them as their other parent did. They are grieving too. The changes for all of you will be difficult.

Children also mourn, each in his or her own way. They can only absorb and process so much information at a time, so they'll be going through emotional adjustments of their own. They will miss the parent who was primary in their life most. Therefore, a mother who had been at home a lot will be missed more than a father who worked long hours and seldom ate with the family.

Children can also be greatly affected by the behavior of the bereaved parent. It is especially bad for them if the surviving parent becomes withdrawn and unapproachable. They need to talk, cry and work on their personal grief.

Death is the final abandonment. The greatest subconscious fear that kids have is that they will lose you too. The best thing you can do is to be as honest as possible about what you are experiencing. Children are not stupid; give them credit. Value their love; respect their feelings.

They can be a great source of comfort to you if you let them.

They will want to help. Let them do as much as they are capable of doing. Don't shut them out or push them away; you are all in this together. Talk to them, cry with them, share with them your feelings of sadness and pain, and allow them to do the same.

Remember, they are learning from you, and the more open and honest you are, the more permission they will have to be the same way. Let them know that grief is a process, a healing process, and that it will be easier every day and soon you will all be happy and joyful again.

After a year or so, you are likely to be more relaxed with the kids, less resentful and angry at having to raise them alone. You will all be much stronger for having come through this crisis together.

If your children are adults, it is equally important to include them in your grieving process. Don't expect them to automatically know what you want or need. Ask for it. They cannot read your mind. Take responsibility for getting what you want. It can relieve your hurt and emotional pain, and keeps them from trying to guess what you need from them.

Adult children are grieving too. Losing a parent is a major life event at any age. It is a time when families can come together in a new and wonderfully supportive way. If family communication has been open and caring, mutual support will occur naturally. If not, now is a time to re-establish love and caring for each other, even though your lives may have taken different paths. Don't be afraid to ask for what you need and want.

You can communicate non-verbally by touching. If you want a hug, ask for it. If you don't want to be alone at some particular time, call someone up and ask them to come and stay with you.

If you need some time away from your kids, ask a friend or relative to keep them overnight. It is important to ask for what you want. You may not always get what you ask for when you need it. But if you learn to do this and take the risk, you will benefit because you asked. The worst thing that can happen is that you may feel a little rejected and angry if the person says no. No big deal!

If you think you need help in communicating better, take a course in assertiveness or effectiveness training. Try your local community college or other adult education classes.

The penalty for not asking for what you want is to become either passive and manipulative, or angry and aggressive. The first is hidden and covert; the second is openly hostile and overt. Neither is effective. Eventually people see through your methods and avoid you.

There is far more pain, hurt, and disappointment in life by being unassertive than by being assertive. There is no doubt: being assertive is risky. You will find out pretty fast who your true friends are, and you may choose to eliminate a few people from your life, but that would happen sooner or later anyway. A true friend is interested in what is best for you and will not abandon you in your time of need. A false friend will flee – and good riddance!

I remember a story that a wise old woman told me years ago, when I was a young bride and worried about my house being spic-and-span when visitors came, which was difficult because I worked full-time. She said, "If someone wants to criticize you, they will find a way. Friends come to see *you* – not your house. Enemies come to see your house – not you." It was such a relief to be free of trying so hard to get the approval of others and to just be me.

Sometimes widows lean too heavily on sons or daughters and/or extended family, thinking they will take care of them, like the spouse once did. This insecurity is the result of a deep fear and dread of not being able to take care of oneself. It is the deprived-child part in all of us that is dependent and wants the best of what our mother was. We want to be nurtured, loved, supported, and to have all of our basic needs met, especially when we are hurting.

Other people may be willing to provide that kind of care for a while, and spend extra time with you, but they will soon resent your dependence. After a while they will withdraw from you, even avoid you, and you will be forced to come to terms with finding a way to begin to take care of yourself. Occasionally, adult children may be too protective of you. Be aware if this happens and make your independence clear.

After a few months, you will come to full realization that your relationships with relatives and friends have changed. In-laws will become less important (except possibly as grandparents). You may become closer to your own relatives temporarily, until you establish your new priorities and identity. Typically some married friends will not continue to be close and intimate with you when you are not part of a "couple." This may be a source of some disappointment, regret and anger.

The best thing to do is to establish new relationships and find new friends as soon as you can. Many communities have programs for widowed people. Check out the one in your town and take time to talk to other folks with similar experiences. Such programs generally have talks by speakers with practical information on legal issues, trust funds, investment possibilities, etc. Some also provide social activities to meet other widows or widowers, activities such as taking trips or going to concerts.

Some have group counseling and crisis intervention. These groups were started to help people like you. Take advantage of them. Though you may not feel very "social," you'll find that talking with others in similar circumstances helps ease your pain.

Like it or not, this is the time of your life to learn to stand on your own two feet, to learn to become self sufficient, to become your own person. Anything and everything you can do to discover and maintain your own personal power will make your future life run much more smoothly.

Set New Goals for Yourself

When a year or so has passed, use this time to figure out what it is that you want your life to be like now, six months from now, one year from now, five years from now – then go after it. During this year, you will begin to formulate plans for your new life. Jean told me, one year after her husband died suddenly of a heart attack, "I can go where I want, when I want to. I don't have to answer to anyone. For the first time in my life, I am really free. I have no desire to marry again. I like my life just the way it is."

Many women at first prefer the company of other widows, their children, and their grandchildren. By the beginning of the second year after the loss, your expectations are clearer and your interests will be broader. You know what you have to do to survive and will already be doing it. Leisure time activities will be more pleasant. You may travel, play golf or tennis, or go backpacking. You will begin to make plans, to think about the future.

Brady, a widowed friend of sixty-three, discovered backpacking after his wife's death, something he had never done before. Now he hikes with a group of single people every Sunday. He has made new friends, gets exercise, and has discovered some special activities of his own that he did not share with his former spouse. She is not in his thoughts as much as if they had enjoyed backpacking together.

New Abilities

By the second year of widowhood, you won't feel so helpless. You will be more in control of your life. Many people find they have strengths and talents that they never realized they had before. Widowed women, especially those who had never made decisions about business or money, find that they are able to get the information and facts necessary to buy and sell property, invest in the stock market, borrow money, and make other business decisions. People are generally very willing to answer your questions. Don't hesitate to call or visit your banker, lawyer, or insurance agent.

You'll learn to maintain the car, make home repairs, etc.,

or at least know how to arrange for these services. Make a list of what you need to know and ask all the questions you have until you thoroughly understand. Or go to your public or college library and ask more questions. Read books or take courses that will enlighten you. The more informed you are, the more independent you become. The more you make informed decisions that are in your own best interest, the more control you can exercise over your life. Use others as consultants and resources – but make your own decisions. Empower yourself!

Meg is a good example. After studying the market and seeking business advice, she opened a dress shop fourteen months after her husband's death, even though she had never worked before. She arranged for a college student to live in and help with her three young children, the housework, and the cooking. Her store is so successful that she is considering opening a second store in a new shopping mall.

Meg says she has never felt so busy and involved and happy. She still thinks of Bill, her dead husband, but he is on her mind less and less. Meg has found new parts of herself that were dormant until she was forced to make decisions on her own about survival for herself and her children. She says that she has learned more about life, herself, and business in the past year than she learned in the thirty-eight years she lived before her husband's death. Many widows become interested in a family business and develop strong executive abilities by filling their husband's shoes.

Letting Go

Many widows and widowers continue to wear their wedding rings during the first year of mourning. The ring is a signal to the world that they are not yet ready to pursue other relationships. It is also a form of denial and an indication of the continuing emotional connection to the dead spouse. The ring must go eventually – the sooner the better – just as the clothes in the closet and other personal items of the deceased must go.

The ring is a symbolic link with the past. To successfully build a new life, you must relinquish the past. Don't force yourself to take off the ring until you are ready, but pay attention to any emotions that you have connected to the ring. And when you are ready, put it away for good. One widow I know wore the ring on a chain around her neck for a few months after she took it off her finger. Then it went into a safety deposit box to be passed on to her daughter when she was older.

The idyllic image of your former relationship will slowly fade. Reality gradually emerges and you begin to remember that your spouse had flaws as well as positive and beautiful aspects.

Len's wife was an alcoholic. At first, after she died, he could only remember her as a beautiful woman, the mother of his children. After about ten months, he was willing to admit how relieved he was not to have to put up with her lies about drinking, her unpredictable behavior at home and at business parties, and the terrible arguments that they had when she was drunk. He was even able to express his anger and disappointment in not having a quality of love in the marriage that might have been there if she had not been an alcoholic.

After a year or so, if your spouse is still in your thoughts daily, you are stuck in your grieving process. It is important for you to begin to let go. If you are still holding on, try this exercise. Lie down and relax completely. Imagine that your mate is lying on the floor with you. Try to pick him or her up every time you get up. Carry him/her with you as you cook, shop, work ... everywhere. You are exhausted. The weight is unbearable ... you have no strength or energy left for anything or anyone else in your life. Now lay the person down and say goodbye with love and let go. Notice your feelings. If tears come, let them out. Repeat the exercise until the emotions are resolved and you can stand calmly alone.

Another very effective way to complete the unfinished business of the relationship is to write a letter to your spouse; it is a way to finish old feelings and conversations that you carry around in your head. Write a letter to say goodbye. Tell all of your feelings of sadness, frustration, anger, and resentment at being left alone. Express love, regret and whatever else you want to tell her or him.

This letter is for your eyes only unless you choose to share it, though you may not. It may take several days to finish it. If feelings come to the surface, allow yourself to experience them. The final purpose of the letter is to release your spouse with love.

Take off the ring. Put away the pictures. Throw away or give away the rest of the clothes. Let go! You will feel much lighter. You'll be free to go on with your own life.

Begin to think of yourself as happy and fulfilled. You are whole. What changes need to be made? Lose weight –

spruce up the house – new clothes? If you would like a new body image, improve it. Your body is the only one you get, so it's important to take care of it. Grieving takes a toll on your physical health. The stress of grieving must be short-term, or serious chronic disease may set in. If your health is bad and you are still preoccupied with thoughts of your spouse, try professional help.

As time goes on, heavy emotional reactions will be experienced less and less often. Anger, resentment, guilt, anxiety, and fears of not being able to survive on your own will become part of the past now.

New Friendships

Some of your new friends will have had similar experiences. Together, you can move into your new lives. Start sharing leisure activities or special interests with new people. Get involved in life.

If you are working, you will be better at managing your time and responsibilities. If you have dependent children at home, they will also begin to come to terms with the changes in the family. You all will probably feel occasional twinges of depression and wish that things could be as they were before, but these times will become fewer and farther between.

Dating

You may have had little interest in dating. But in the second year, you may begin seriously searching for a new love. Your relationships will become more authentic, deeper, more open and more trusting. The men or women who interest you now may be quite different from your dead spouse. Earlier you may have been attracted to someone who was similar to him/her in some way. Perhaps a subconscious effort to replace him/her was at work.

Now, after a few years, you have grown and changed, and a different type of person may be more attractive to you. You may feel that if you had a chance to remarry your husband/wife again, you would not do so. After all, the circumstances of the death forced you to change, to get out in the world and become more independent. You are not necessarily attracted to the same type of person. Your attitudes and values are always changing. Being open to new opportunities and new lifestyles is what living is all about.

If you become interested in someone or some activity that you know your former spouse would disapprove of, you may have a few minutes of guilt, as if he or she were looking over your shoulder. Forget it. The past is over: past. You are the one responsible for your life now. Let go of that old tape that says you *should* do things in the old way. You are not the old you anymore. You are the new you and only you can make your own decisions.

Sexuality

Younger widows and widowers are more likely to begin to seek sexual activity sooner and more frequently than older people. Sometimes there is a period of promiscuity, of searching for validation and self-worth through sexual encounters. Sometimes there is a strong desire to be physically close, to touch and be touched. Another desire is to psychologically fill the empty spot in your heart and your bed through the intimacy of sexual intercourse. When you are looking for love and only get sex, you may be disappointed and regret the whole adventure. But before long you will try again.

Sexuality and the desire for sexual satisfaction are part of a lifelong pattern. Health and the availability of a willing partner are more important than age. If an active and satisfying sex life with your former partner was important, then it will continue to be a priority.

The absence of a regular sexual partner can cause emotional conflict and physical frustration. Dreams may become sensual in nature, even to the point of being orgasmic. They may even include images of sexual relations with your children or friends, and if this happens there is no need to feel shocked or ashamed. These people generally represent some aspect of the lost relationship, or some area of deprivation in your current situation.

It is a good practice to masturbate, if this is within your personal moral code. Masturbation can have several positive benefits: it is a good way to relieve physiological tension; it is an excellent and fast way to cope with frustration; it is a way to nurture yourself. It may also be the sexual release that can prevent you from becoming involved with someone else before you are ready. Remember, this is a time of extreme vulnerability, and it is very easy to make decisions or choices that may not be in your own best interest in the long run. Go slowly and carefully in the beginning.

Sexual frustration alone should not lead you into a new relationship, especially with any hopes for it to last forever. Companionship is fine, but be aware of how much you are substituting a new person for your dead mate.

Lisa started dating three months after her husband died. At first she was concerned about being with a new man, afraid that she might not do or say the right things, or even know what would be expected of her. Lisa chose as her first partner a man who "had a beard and looked just like Jim." The relationship was not right for her; it lasted for only a few months. However, it got her through that difficult first encounter with another person of the opposite sex.

Keep in mind, too, that there are unscrupulous people who consider you good prey, and for selfish motives want to use you sexually, and/or get money you may inherit. You may yearn for love and support, but it is better to give it to yourself for now, while you are vulnerable.

Remarriage

Older men and women tend to take longer to begin seeking a new mate. Women, especially those who evaluate their chances of remarriage and decide it is unlikely, choose – rather than to compete with younger women for the few available men – to simply give up any idea of vigorously searching for another mate. Men, on the other hand, almost always remarry within a short period of time. Men flourish with a woman to meet their sexual and other physical needs. Of course, men have more options than women. There are more available females in most age groups. However, both men and women may choose other options besides marriage, including women who find relationships with younger men.

Many women have told me that although they loved their husbands, they would never marry again and serve the needs of another. One widow put it this way. She said, "I served my time. I raised three children. My husband was a good man. When he died, I was lost for over a year. But now I'm happy. This is my time for me." This is borne out in the time frame for remarriage.

Widows who remarry do so a little after four years on the average, while widowers remarry within two years.

Age is a significant factor in remarriage for a widow. Young women under the age of twenty-four tend to remarry within one year. Some widows report that they do not wish to ever marry again, but many do. The older the woman is when she is widowed, the less her chances are of finding a suitable new mate.

By age sixty-five, only thirty percent of women are married, as opposed to seventy percent of men. Middle age years are those when many people become widowed. Widows under thirty years have the best opportunity to remarry. The majority of women widowed during the middle years, ages thirty-five to fifty-four, often remarry if they find a suitable partner.

After the Second Year

By now you may have decided to relocate to a new home or town, gone back to school, or taken a job. It is likely that you have found a new love or mate by now, or have arranged your sex life in a way that no longer causes a conflict. You have some new friends that are a support system for you and someone with whom you can go out for dinner and a movie. Relationships with your children and family have settled down. Your self-esteem is intact, and life in general is more satisfying.

CHAPTER FIVE

DEATH OF PARENTS

Adults of young to middle age are the generation "in the middle" between their older parents and their younger children, and with varying degrees of responsibility and dependency to both. Generally, some time in mid-life one or both parents die, and the adult children become the elders of the family.

The key issues that determine how the death of a parent will affect an adult child are: the nature of the relationship with that parent; the age of the child when the death occurs; the emotional maturity of the surviving child; the length of time of warning prior to the death; and the time the parent and child have spent discussing both the practical and emotional aspects involved in the parent's death.

Obviously, the older and more mature the son or daughter is, the longer the time of warning, the more open the relationship between parent and child, the easier it will be to process the grief for a dead parent. When a young child loses a parent, or the death is sudden, or the relationship is tense, the grief may remain unresolved for years.

The stages of recovery and the processes of grieving after the death of a parent are usually not as disabling or intense as when you lose a spouse, lover, or child. Parents are expected to die before their children, so to some extent we're all prepared for our parents to die. Not that it is ever easy to lose a significant emotional relationship, but most of us hold a prevailing notion that it is just or appropriate when death comes to someone who is older and has had a chance to live long enough to complete some or all of the tasks of the life cycle. It's much easier to accept this kind of loss without the sense of injustice that comes up when a child or younger adult dies.

Lingering Dependency on Parents

The age of the child when his parent dies influences how well he will handle the grief. For a small child, the death of a parent is a mystery. The child will often have feelings of guilt and think that he caused the death by some "bad" or naughty act. Or he may be possessed by a fear of being abandoned or punished.

Joan lost her mother in a typhoid epidemic when she was five years old. Three weeks later, her older brother died of the same disease. Joan was too young to understand death. She only knew her mother had died and gone away. That traumatic loss created in Joan lifelong fears of losing someone she loved through death. Her anxiety grew over the years and finally manifested itself in the fear of losing herself, in fearing her own death. Every time a friend, acquaintance or family member got seriously ill or died, Joan would panic and feel that she would soon become sick and die.

As a vulnerable five-year old, she was too young to understand her loss, and some of its mystery lingered in her mind. Because her mother and brother died of an illness, any illness in her life triggered those same feelings of fear and dread at losing someone critical to her survival. Finally, after short-term counseling, Joan was able to recognize the anxiety feelings as they arose and to replace them with positive thoughts and feelings. Eventually, she was able to complete the grieving process by acknowledging her love for her mother and letting go of the dependency she still felt as a holdover from her childhood.

A child is vulnerable at any age when a parent dies. If the parent-child relationship has never progressed to an adult-to-adult relationship, then all of the childhood fears of being abandoned will be reactivated, no matter how old the child is. The same feelings may be experienced at the death of a stepparent, grandparent or guardian who was a significant person in the child's upbringing.

Vera was fifty-six years old when her mother died of a sudden heart attack. She always loved and respected her mother as the elder person of authority and power. Even though Vera was a grandmother herself, she acted like a little girl when she was around her mother; even her voice changed to that of a little girl. When her mother died, Vera felt totally abandoned and lost – as a little child might feel. She was devastated by the death. She developed a gastric ulcer, and had one bout after another with the flu. The stress of losing her mother compromised her immune system. She was virtually unable to conduct her life in a normal way during her grieving period. Finally, after seeking help, she realized that she was no longer a child, but an adult. As she accepted this, she became stronger and more self-assured. Her extreme dependency lessened and she was able to release her mother in a healthy way. At a recent wedding in the family, Vera assumed the role of matriarch, replacing her mother in the family hierarchy.

The death of a parent is a particularly profound loss when a child identifies very strongly with the parent who dies. Often the remaining parent becomes the target of resentment, anger and other strong feelings.

Consider Roger, who felt a strong connection with and respect for his father. When the father died after a long and painful illness, Roger, an engineer who worked in another state, felt guilty about not being around to ease the pain of his father's last year alive.

His father was outgoing, successful in business, and had many friends. Roger was just the opposite: quiet, introverted, and with few friends. In Roger's mind, his father could do no wrong. In addition to idealizing his father he mistrusted his mother.

He became convinced that she did not support his dying father the way he would have. He blamed his mother for his father's illness and eventual death. Instead of grieving for his father, Roger generalized his hatred of his mother to all women, a feeling he carried for ten years. He is now forty-three years old, has never married and has had only one relationship with a woman. That woman was thirty-three years his senior, nearly the age of his grandmother, the only woman he ever trusted.

Years later, Roger is still carrying around a connection with his father and is stuck in the first stage of denial.

Roger will not complete the recovery process and get on with his own life until he accepts the differences between himself and his father. Eventually, Roger must come to terms with remembering his father realistically. He must see that his father was a normal man with faults. Roger must then accept the fact of his father's death.

Psychologically, he must bury his father before he can move into the position of the man in the family, or in any relationship, a role he feels inadequate to fill.

A parent's death can exacerbate other emotional crises going on in a child's life at the same time.

In the movie "Middle Age Crazy," the death of his father is one of the events that trigger the forty-year-old protagonist's fling with irresponsibility. His own aging, his son's departure for college, heavy business responsibilities – and the death of the family patriarch – leave the character pleading, "But I don't want to be the Daddy." So he runs away from his home and has an affair with a cheerleader in an effort to fight off the fast mounting responsibilities of age.

Because the parent-child roots are so deep, there may be bonds that remain long after the parent has died, as with Roger. Sometimes a child will endeavor to fulfill the uncompleted fantasies or dreams of a parent.

Marge, for example, was the oldest of five children. Her father treated her as the son he wanted for the first six years of her life, until the first son was born. Then gradually, as the boy grew big enough to accompany his father on hunting and fishing trips, as Marge had done in the past, her brother replaced her as the close companion of their father.

Marge was twenty-three when her father's sudden death jolted the entire family. A few years later, she applied for law school. She had always planned to become an attorney because that was her father's unfulfilled lifelong dream. She was trying to become something for him that he never became.

She reported great surprise at her feelings of relief and being "off the hook" when she was turned down for admission to law school. When she finally went to graduate school, she followed her own areas of interest, which were not related to law.

At a subconscious level, she had still wanted to please her father and win back the love she felt she was denied after her brother was born. Feeling relieved clued her into the fact that she needed to deal further with her father's death, and it helped her get on with her own life.

When the identification with one parent is greater than with the other, the death of that parent naturally has more impact on the child. It also presents a perfect opportunity to confront oneself about buried emotions. If the grieving process is handled completely, in practical and psychological terms, the child can move to new areas of growth and maturity. The death of a parent is a chance to progress, not regress.

Clearing up Old Business

In western society, where many of our relationships are full of superficial courtesy, there is often a great deal of unfinished "business" when a parent dies. The relationships that are the hardest to clean up and be open and honest about are those charged with emotional content. They are those relationships in which we feel that we have the most to lose if we are honest about our feelings and values and attitudes. Consequently, parents and children may continue to play old roles for years and never treat each other as adults.

I have known people in their forties who are afraid to smoke a cigarette in front of their parents, although they smoke regularly in their daily lives. They argue that they are trying to protect their parents' feelings and respect their position about smoking. Yet their relationship with their parents is dishonest: they are really trying to protect themselves from their Mommy's or Daddy's disapproval. They are not secure enough and mature enough to risk disapproval by declaring their independence as adults.

Parents are our first authority figures. When a parent in such a relationship dies, a child may be relieved that she won't have to be phony any longer. But quickly following the relief, she feels guilty for feeling relieved! So she is not free. Because the relationship was inauthentic and superficial, the child remained a child, letting her parent's values determine her behavior.

She has to complete her own maturing process of becoming a separate independent adult after the parent's death. That may be just as hard to do as when the parent was alive. And if the child can't step out on her own, she may permit the dead parent to continue to have the power of approval and disapproval over her behavior for the rest of her life.

Adolescence is the typical time to make a break with parental values, attitudes, and power. But if, as an adult, you still haven't fully made the break, I urge you to do so as soon as possible. It is much more difficult after the parent is dead to break with the parental values and become an independent and self-sufficient person.

Cleaning up relationships with parents can feel extremely frightening and threatening, especially when you know that they disapprove of something that's part of you. One of the best ways is to be sure of what you really have to say or do to feel free and independent. Name calling and blaming sessions can be avoided if you know what you want to convey to your parent. Spontaneous eruptions of anger and hostility accomplish little and can drive a wedge between you and your parents.

Think through clearly what you want your parents to understand. Then rehearse in your imagination a scene where you tell them. Notice, as you rehearse, any fears, feelings of frustration or anger, or other emotions that you are experiencing. Pay attention to your body also. Be aware of any areas of physical stress, like stomachache, cramps, headache, changes in breathing, tension along your spine, etc. Most likely you will re-experience old chronic areas of physical tension that you established long ago as a response to childhood fears of the adult authority figures that your parents represented.

As you rehearse and get in touch with emotional and physical tensions and fears, acknowledge them and then let go of them. This may take some effort on your part. Keep going over the same scene until you can do it without any feeling or reaction. It may take several tries, but don't give up. If you get stuck, talk it over with a therapist.

Sometimes, if the issues on which you disagree are too serious, it may be wiser or easier to finish old business using other methods, such as writing a letter you never mail, but saying all of the things you wanted to get off your chest and never did. However, it's best to get professional advice before deciding against a confrontation.

Only after you have completed this rehearsal and planning process should you approach your parents with the issues that you want to clear up. Then make an appointment. Tell them you have something serious that you want to talk to them about, and ask when it's convenient for them to talk to you. If you can predict the amount of time it will take, tell them this too. If you set the agenda or the topic of conversation and the length of time you are willing to be with them, then you are the one in control of the situation. Most important, you have defused the emotional bomb for yourself. After the first step, things get easier. So you will be able to direct the conversation, and not be subject to getting hooked into old ways of being manipulated.

When you meet with your parents, start by giving them some idea of what you want to talk about. A few introductory words – such as, "This is hard for me to say but I want to do it because it's important to be honest with you," – will give them notice that you intend to assert yourself and are serious about it.

Then be direct and factual with your message. The simplest way is the best. My friend, the smoker, might say to her parents something like this: "Mother and Dad, I want to tell you that I smoke cigarettes and have for years. I am tired of hiding the fact from you. I intend to continue to smoke at the present time. If you disapprove of my smoking, as I fear you do, I hope that you will not disapprove of me. And if you do, then I regret losing your love for now, but I have to be true to myself."

The more serious the matter of disagreement is, the more difficult it will be to discuss with your parents. Telling a staunchly anti-divorce parent that your marriage is over, or a hopeful grandmother that you've decided not to have children, may seem cruel. But it's probably unkind not to face the issue and to leave your parents wondering or hoping and yourself guilt-ridden. A son who decides not to enter the family business, as his father has always assumed he would do, is dealing with very important values. One of the hardest moments is to reveal homosexuality to a parent who is horrified by such an idea.

Your parents will naturally follow the long-established patterns of dealing with you – saying no, scolding, threatening punishment. These first reactions could even extend to vowing to cut you out of the will, or threatening to withdraw their love in some way. However, if you are prepared for the worst, then their threats will not work this time. You are standing on your own feet. No matter what the cost, you will have made a major step toward reclaiming your own self and to growing up.

The most common parental response is to try the old

ways to control you, as when you were their young child. When they realize that it is not working anymore, they will most often relent and accept you as you are.

It may take them a little while to come to terms with the changes in your relationship. Give them all the time they need. Remember that you needed time to be able to gain the courage to confront the issue yourself. Offer them time to think about it, and when they are ready and want to discuss the issues further, be available to do so. If your parent is disappointed in you, it is beyond your control. You've made your step toward redefining the relationship. It's now up to your parents to adjust their expectations.

For your parents, accepting the change may be difficult. They've been used to the old ways perhaps longer than you have. They may greet the news with silence – a form of denial – and may simply decline to talk about it any further. On the other hand, your folks may surprise you and be far more receptive than you expect.

Keep your options open. Few parents are willing to lose contact with their children, and in time they will come around to accepting the changes in you and the changes in your relationship with them. Remember, change is always difficult, particularly where emotions are involved. It requires giving up familiar ways of doing things. Even if the old ways didn't work and weren't honest, they were comfortable, familiar and easy, like an old pair of slippers with holes in the toes.

Old ways are comfortable. You may have a twinge of sadness at throwing away "old friends." But the old ways must go to make way for new ones. Sometimes the scary part is that you may not know what the new ways of relating to your parents are yet, and since you know the old ways, the old slippers, it may feel safer and less risky to hang on to them.

But it's worthwhile and exciting to move on to new levels of maturity. The second hurdle is still high, but easier than the first.

Once an open dialogue is started with your parents, it is easier to keep it that way. The benefits can be enormous. You can begin to relate to each other as real human beings. You learn new things about each other and you may find a depth of love that you never knew was there.

Diane resented her mother for years. Every time Diane would move to a new city, her mother would follow within six months. Her mother was becoming more disabled with respiratory disease and made increasing demands on Diane's time and energy. Prior to the last move, Diane felt angry and resentful. She worked up her courage and told her mother what she was feeling. Both of them were upset for a while. But in the process of talking about the feelings and the alternatives available, both women came to terms with the reality of the situation. Diane and her mother worked out a solution that was comfortable for both.

Her mother moved to the new town, and Diane found her a two-bedroom apartment, then hired a live-in housekeeper to stay in the second bedroom. Diane visited often and took her mother to the doctor and shopping. In the process of working it out, both women were able to deal with the impending death of the mother and be supportive of each other. They became closer than they had ever been, and often both of them were able to express sincere and deep love for each other.

Being able to discuss your parent's health or approaching death is important in being able to finish business between you and say goodbye. But it takes an honesty that must be prepared for by honesty about other matters and feelings.

After a Parent Dies

If your parent is already dead, it is, of course, harder to come to terms with the problematic issues in the relationship, because a face-to-face encounter is no longer possible. If you find that sorting out the issues is too difficult to do on your own, then see a professional counselor or psychotherapist. Usually, short-term counseling can help you become unstuck and let go of the chains of the past.

Unfinished business with parents is a constant theme I hear from clients. The role of a parent, especially of the mother, has been damned and criticized and made very difficult by changing sex roles and shifting family structures in recent years. If she encouraged self-sufficiency and independence in her children, she may be accused of being cold, distant, or unfeeling. If she was warm and loving, she may be called smothering and manipulative. Parenting is a paradox.

The biggest single way to make progress in grieving for a dead parent, or to work out your relationship with a live parent, is to recognize what a difficult job it is to be a parent. Praise them for their victories and forgive them for their trespasses, mistakes, and failures. Take the same attitude toward yourself. No one is perfect. You were not perfect as a child and, fortunately, you do not have to be perfect now as an adult. Be gentle and loving toward yourself and to others in your life – living or dead.

Sometimes a son or daughter will carry around a subconscious belief that he or she will die at the same age as, or before, a beloved parent died. Recently a friend lost her husband at forty-eight years old. At the funeral, I expressed condolences and mentioned his age. My friend told me she wasn't really surprised by his heart attack and sudden death.

Her husband always said that he would die before he was fifty because his father had died at that age. Clearly, this man could not outdo his father by outliving him, and chose to cut short his life when he did. This is called a family script.

Another friend, Marlene, whose father died at forty-four, began to get her estate in order about a year before her forty-fourth birthday. She made out a will, appointed an executor of her estate, joined a memorial society, selected the music to be played at her funeral, made arrangements to donate her body organs, and had long discussions with her children about who wanted which keepsakes.

She was extremely busy at the time, teaching and preparing for an international trip, but she was driven to complete these tasks. As the time got closer to her birthday and to the anniversary of her father's death, she developed severe anxiety and could not explain her pervasive feelings of fear.

Finally, she went to a counselor and realized that she

had never completed the grieving process for her father. She had only buried, and repressed, her pain and anger at him for dying and leaving her. Subconsciously she still wanted to be with him, and so she set herself to complete her life at the same time that his life ended. Counseling helped her see what she was doing, and soon she was able to finally bury him, psychologically. She was relieved to pass her birthday uneventfully.

When the grieving process is not effectively dealt with for one parent, the death of the second parent often presents us with an opportunity to complete the process for both parents. When both parents have died, the transition from child to adult, from middle generation to older generation, is completed.

Sometimes there is also a feeling that one life replaces another. In my own family, a niece was born two weeks after the death of her grandfather, and the celebration of welcoming the new child was bittersweet: the grieving was also relieved by joy at the new life.

Another common phenomenon, especially in marriages of many years, is for one spouse to die shortly after the death of a beloved mate, often within a year. The children are faced with the death of both parents in a short period of time. If the couple is very old, the survivor may feel a profound sense of loneliness and have little desire to rebuild a new life. For the widowed one, the wish to join the dead partner becomes so obsessive that he chooses or "wills" himself to die.

Such people truly die from a broken heart when death occurs with no apparent physical cause. We know so little scientifically about the will to live and the will to die; yet many of us are familiar with this phenomenon. We all know someone, directly or indirectly, who willed to live, fighting incredible odds to survive, or willed to die, and perished of no discernible cause.

Afterwards

After the funeral, life returns to normal for most people. If, however, you lived in the same house with your parent, then his absence will leave a bigger empty spot and adjustments will have to be made to change daily habits and established routines.

Emotionally, there may be feelings of sadness, anger, depression, and even relief, especially after a long illness that has been painful for the parent and stressful for the family. The emotional responses when a parent dies are generally less acute than with other deaths, and grief is resolved in a shorter period of time, usually six months to a year.

If the parent and children related to each other as independent adults, self-esteem and identity issues are less significant when a parent dies. Frequently, adult children have left the nest and made a life of their own, and don't have constant daily contact with their parents.

Soon after the funeral, the demands of work and family and other commitments require the bereaved to return to the routines of family life, and the parent's death is pushed or forced into the background.

The death of a parent has the potential for good and bad feelings among sisters and brothers. Property settlement issues can take years to resolve. A clear, explicit will on the part of the parent can help to reduce such difficulties. That is one reason to talk about these things *before* the death. Afterwards it may be too late.

A parent's death can be the occasion for a renewal of closeness between siblings. Yet sometimes brothers and sisters drift away from each other after their parents die. Political and life-style differences tend to increase the gap. The ongoing love, support, and caring of the large family of aunts, uncles, and cousins is quickly becoming a thing of the past except in a few small communities, and where kinship and religious ties are strong.

The childless adult often feels truly orphaned if left without any family. He needs to increase friendships and close relationships to assure an ongoing support system.

The death of parents often brings up feelings of our own deaths as we take on the role of family elders. Sometimes there is no one to pass the guard to. It may be sad to imagine leaving no new generation behind, even if one has chosen not to have children.

It's important to keep these feelings in perspective during the grieving process. We can't guarantee the future, just as we can't change the past. Succession of generations and the conflicting emotions of grief will soon come into proper focus again, as you return to your normal life.

Grandchildren

The death of parents may bring you closer to your own children, as you realize that in the normal cycle of life you will someday leave them behind. Grandchildren also grieve for their loss. The severity of grief depends on the closeness of the relationship with the grandparent and the age of the grandchild.

One important aspect is that the death of a grandparent brings the child closer to the reality of the future death of parents. Often, losing a grandparent is the first loss by death a child experiences. The way parents handle their own grief becomes a model for children in processing losses through death in the future. If the child had a close intimate relationship with the grandparent, the death could be devastating to the young child.

If the grandchildren are adults when a grandparent dies, they are often the best and closest support their parent has. I asked my grown son how he felt when his grandmother, my mother, died. He said, "I felt a little sad for myself but relieved for you." My mother had been ill for several years before her death. He was able to see the stress her illness had produced for me.

CHAPTER SIX

DEATH OF CHILREN

The death of a child, especially one's own child, is something the mind can hardly comprehend. It seems to go against nature. The end of a life that is still forming or has just begun is an almost unthinkable cruelty.

But it happens. Parents sometimes must witness the illness or suffering and eventual death of the children to whom they gave birth. And those parents must go on living. They may have other children to care for; they may become parents again later. While nothing will ever fill the empty place that the departed child leaves behind, life goes on for the child's mother and father. Even if your child is gone, you still have a future, as gray and worthless as it may at first seem.

No matter the age of the child, whether the death occurs as a baby, young person, adolescent or adult, the feelings are devastating. Your role as a parent is to love, protect, teach and nurture your child. Parents expect to die before their children.

It is the natural order of life events. When the situation is reversed, and a child dies before the parents, it seems wrong.

Yet we never know why one person dies and another lives. We do know that the bereaved survivors must remain and heal and go on with their life. Though death may take your child, the love never goes away.

The grief after a child's death is one of the longest and hardest types of loss to live with. It's necessary to cope with your own emotions and those of other family members. Sometimes when a child has a lingering illness, you also have to deal with his or her suffering.

Death of a Child through Illness

Cancer, leukemia, and other forms of malignancy are the reasons for most deaths by illness of young children. When the child and the parents are forewarned of the coming death, there is an opportunity to work through some of the pain of separation and loss before death occurs. But not every parent does this. Some hang onto hope and stay in denial until the last breath has been taken.

The question always comes up whether or not to tell a child that he or she is dying. The age of the child is a major consideration in this decision. If she is three years old or more, the truth must be told in a way that she can understand. Using an age appropriate story helps relate previous experiences with death. Perhaps a puppy or a goldfish died, or a bird or a distant relative. Referring to that situation will be helpful in explaining the present situation to her. Religious ideas or some concept he is curious about can be fit into an explanation of what is happening in your child's life.

The death of a child forces parents to come to terms with their understanding of the *meaning* of death. This is basically what they *try* to explain to the child – not just the facts of death, but some idea of its meaning in religious or spiritual or philosophical terms. That explanation must be given in terms the individual child can relate to.

For example, Jim, a bright eight-year-old, had a fatal kidney disease. His favorite subject in school was mathematics. He had asked his parents several times about the last number ... the very *last* number. "I can count to 100, 1,000, 10,000 and more, but what is the last number?" he would ask. His mother told him that numbers didn't end, the last number was called infinity, which just went on and on. But Jim didn't understand. When he kept asking about the *last* number, his mother finally said that she didn't know ... the only one who might know is God. When his parents finally got up the courage to tell Jim about his illness and upcoming death, he said, "Well, now maybe I can find out about the *last* number. When I get to heaven, I will ask God what infinity is."

Jim was typical in his response. Usually the child knows at some level of consciousness that his illness is serious. But the meaning of death to a child will be limited to personal experience and to stories that he may have heard from friends or read in books.

Separation from parents is the closest feeling to death

a very young child can relate to. Separation anxiety is a prevailing fear of loss, usually of the mother. Young children will relate to death in these terms, in terms of going away, of leaving, of being alone. They won't feel the sadness or depth of meaning as profoundly as their parents will.

Parents may be worried about breaking down and crying in front of the child. But tears, sadness, and other emotions are natural and real. Putting on a brave, stoic front will not only be phony, but can encourage the child to try to behave the same way and not feel free to cry and express real feelings.

Most reports from dying children (and adults) reveal that they want and feel comfortable with reality and truth, sincerity and honesty. Phoniness is confusing and energy-draining. It cheats the dying person of the right to complete the business of life honestly and realistically. Promises of "when you get better," and "when you come home," when everybody *knows* that the child is dying and will never go home are patronizing and keep up phony pretenses.

Children are sensitive to non-verbal signals. They know when you are hedging or being dishonest. If your words do not match your facial expression or what your body reveals, it is confusing to your child. She will know when you are lying. Children take the clues for their behavior from your behavior. Be open and responsive with your words and your actions.

Feel free to express love, sadness and any other emotions as they arise, so your child can feel free to express his feelings too.

Answer all of the child's questions as openly and honestly as you can. If you don't know the answer, find out. Your doctor and hospital staff are employed by you; you are paying for their services. You do not need their approval of what *you* tell *your* child. Be assertive in requesting that they be honest with your child and about any special services or considerations you may want or need.

After you have told your child the truth in language he or she can understand, it is important to let the child's own natural grieving process take over. Age, personality, and patterns of handling stress and change will dictate how your child will work it out. Remember, the child's way will probably not be your way, so let the child do it *his* or *her* way.

A quiet, shy child may not want to talk about it or let any of her friends know. An outgoing boy may want to continue to play Little League baseball as long as possible. A teen-ager may want to live long enough to go to the prom. From grade school on, friends' attitudes become increasingly important. Help your child to continue to live as normally as possible. Keeping relationships with friends and schoolmates will make the final months and days easier.

Sometimes when radical drug therapy (chemotherapy) is used, there are side effects, such as causing the patient's hair to fall out. This can be very difficult for a child to accept. Surgery, scars, tumors, open wounds, and other disfiguring physical changes will require special caring and love and support from family and friends.

Each time something that results in physical change happens, the child will have a separate grieving process.

He will experience little pieces of his death. And each little piece will be mourned. Feelings of denial, anger, frustration, depression, and worry about what his friends will think or say will all come up for him before he will be ready to accept the change. Tell the child you understand these feelings and you love him. Don't try to deny or downplay his distress or he'll have conflicting feelings.

Sometimes parents or neighbors can learn to give injections and other medical treatments that permit the child to stay at home. If your child can spend the last months at home, try to treat the child the way you always have. Let sisters and brothers spend time with the sick one. Let them squabble and play as usual. Children process emotional issues through playing.

If you have been a physically demonstrative family, then continue to touch the dying child as much as or more than before. Touch is a wonderful way to communicate, to show your love and acceptance. Patting, rocking, stroking, washing and combing hair, massaging, and grooming are all good ways to say, "I love you," without words. This is a way for brothers and sisters to be close.

Death of a Child by Accident

"I always felt that the worst thing that could happen to me was for one of my children to die, to be killed. I used to think that I would die too. If someone came to my door or called me on the telephone and said that one of my children was dead, that I would die on the spot. I always wanted to die before any of my children did. I wanted the deaths in our family to be in the right order: first parents, at old age, then the children.

"When my daughter died, I wanted to die for a long time. Sometimes I still do, and that was almost two years ago. When I heard the news of her death, I was immediately in shock. I was numb, floating like in a dream, a nightmare really, that I couldn't wake up from. I seemed to stay that way for a long time ... for months. Then gradually I came out of it, and now I am still alive and Cindy is dead."

Mary Kay, a new member of a Compassionate Friends support group of people who have lost children through death, told her story the first night the group met. Her seventeen-year-old daughter, an honor student, had gone to a party with some friends on the night of their high school graduation. On the way home, their car hit another car head-on. Three of the students were killed, including Cindy, and three others were seriously injured.

In some fatal injuries, there is a little time before the death takes place. This warning time may ease the shock a bit. One family had a few days to adjust to losing a two-year-old son who had accidentally inhaled fumes from paint thinner. He lingered for three days in the hospital as his lung tissues deteriorated. Then he died quietly in his sleep. The parents were numb with disbelief and shock. The child's father, who was with him at the time of the accident, experienced a great deal of guilt because he left the paint thinner within reach of his son.

Those few days that the parents had to get used to the idea of the accident and the possibility of the death gave them a brief head start in their mourning process. As a general rule, the more forewarning you have, the faster the recovery from grief will be, although of course reactions vary from person to person.

Accidents, by their very nature, imply a wrongdoing. When a child dies accidentally, the survivors often feel terrible guilt and blame.

Tony, a four-year-old boy who ran into the street to buy an ice cream from a vendor, was hit by a car, and as he lay dying in the hospital, he kept saying over and over, "I'm sorry, Mommy, don't be mad at me." He had been warned of the dangers of automobiles and told a hundred times not to run into the street, but his impulse for ice cream was greater than his concern for safety.

Tony felt guilty and feared rejection from his parents because he got caught disobeying them. His mother felt guilty because she had given him money to buy the ice cream on his own.

He had on other occasions successfully bought ice cream on his own, under his mother's supervision. Subconsciously, she was furious with him for disobeying her, for doing this to her, for getting hurt and for dying. Her mixed emotions added to her anguish.

The tragedy of a child's accidental death is that it seems so unnecessary and unfair. The child's life has been snuffed out so early, so prematurely. The parents and the driver of the car take a mental snapshot or have a movie in their minds of the incident. They play the film over and over again: wondering, speculating, wishing, planning, thinking, trying to understand, to rearrange events, to change the accident. Trying to live with the loss. Trying to go on and live. Trying to remember and trying to forget all at the same time. Wishing they could mentally will time to move backward, to somehow erase what happened. Wishing it had been you instead of your child. And feeling guilty for being alive. And feeling sorry for yourself that you are. Feeling sorry that you cannot escape the sadness and the loss and the confusion and pain.

When an adult child dies, and his parents survive, the emotions may be just as intense as if they had lost their son or daughter in childhood. The older person wonders, "Why her, when she had so many years ahead? Why not me? I'm old; I've lived." The parents may sincerely wish they could trade places with the dead child.

The Family

Saying goodbye to your child will be one of the hardest tasks you'll ever do. Everyone in the family will be affected by this death. It will seem unbearably painful – but it can also be an opportunity to learn a lot about yourself. Sharing this common experience can be a chance to grow and to become closer to other members of your family. Sometimes life's most painful tasks can be lessons that move us to another place in our development as individuals and as a family.

After the death and the funeral are over, you will need some time to adjust and rest. If you have worked through some of your feelings during the illness, it may be a little easier and somewhat faster for you to recover and to get through your mourning. You will need at least a month or two to break the everyday habits of having that child around. There will be little reminders to keep you remembering, such as toys, clothes, or other personal belongings.

Holidays, photographs, the bedroom, friends from the neighborhood or school, will all hit you with renewed sadness as you realize that your child is gone. Accept these things and let your feelings surface when they are ready. As soon as possible, get rid of as many reminders around the house as you can. Give away the clothes and toys and personal belongings. Put away the photographs for a while. Paint and redecorate the bedroom; get new furniture if possible. You may save one or two things as keepsakes, but put them away for now.

Gradually, you will find yourself letting go of your child as you clear out the old and make room in your life for someone or something new. You will begin to build the next part of your life. Don't force yourself to do these things, but don't delay either. Do them as you feel ready to do them. Each step will lead you closer to acceptance of the death. You are not denying that your child lived; you are helping yourself heal and go on with life.

Slowly, in time, you will notice that you are dwelling on the child less and less. And when you do, the feelings will be less painful. You will start to look forward to things again. When you do think or talk about your dead child, you'll remember both the good and the not-so-good things about her or him. No one is perfect, and it is important to remember your child in a realistic way – in happier, healthier times, as a normal youngster.

The time of recovery will vary from person to person. We are all unique and we grieve in different ways. If you have allowed yourself to cry and to feel your sadness and anger and other feelings, you should begin to accept the reality of the death sometime after six months. If you get stuck, get some counseling. Talk to friends or join a group of parents going through a similar experience. Compassionate

Friends is a good self-help group. There is a lot of comfort in knowing that you are not alone in your grief and pain. You may be able to give some comfort to other people. Helping others is a good way to help yourself.

The role of religion can be important in your grieving process. If you have faith in God or some other power higher than here on earth, or if you believe in reincarnation, you may take a type of comfort in your mourning process from believing that death is not the final end. Religious belief is, of course, an individual matter. For some parents, the tragedy of losing a child has shaken their ability to believe in a just God or a meaning in life. Some people may in time return to their faith. Even if your fundamental beliefs are shaken, you must work through your bitterness and anger.

The first few months after the child's death will be filled with regrets, wishes and feelings, all confused and mixed together in a way that's painful, overwhelming and seemingly unbearable. As the parent, you are torn apart inside. Your mixed and powerful feelings are normal, because you are experiencing one of the most dreaded events that can occur in life. Yet, as impossible as it may seem, you are still alive and you will go on living.

Norma told a group of other bereaved parents who had lost a child, "I was floating in a black void when my daughter was dying. Nothing was real; it was a continual nightmare every day and every night." Other parents understood her experience.

Martha shared her behavior at the funeral: "At my son's funeral I consoled everyone else. I told them all 'It's going to be okay.' I had a need to talk incessantly to anyone who would listen. I drove people away from me. I wore them out."

Many parents need the same loving, listening support. We need time to get it out: to talk, cry, rage and laugh during this time of pain and anguish.

It helps to keep the old patterns of your life going as much as possible. If you have a job, keep working, even part-time. Stay as involved as possible in outside activities. Make a list of people who will listen. Talk with friends and family members about your feelings when you need to. Seeing a professional counselor may be very helpful. Let go of grudges and guilt, and don't blame yourself and others. Nothing is to be gained by holding onto resentment, hate, anger, or hostility.

They won't bring your child back or ease your sense of loss. Such feelings can become barriers between you and others and can cause serious illness in the long run. This is especially important for wives and husbands.

More than ever before, this is the time when family members should be supportive and caring and loving toward each other. Everyone is experiencing a private hell. A death in the family affects all of the members, individually and together. If you have other children they need support and help.

Support, care, and love are nurturing activities. They are something that we usually think of "giving" to someone else, but sometimes we need to make sure we receive this nurturing. In our society, women have been the main nurturers. But when a mother is in deep grief and mourning, she is thrown back on whatever reserve resources she may have to nurture herself to survive, with little or nothing left over to give others. In fact, now is the time that she needs help *from* others.

The father may be in a dreadful state of grief, but unable to express his pain in a direct way. He may start drinking heavily, staying away from home, or he may withdraw into a depression. He may suffer needlessly by resisting the simple but important act of crying. Until recently, men have been neither encouraged nor rewarded for nurturing or for expressing their feelings of doubt and helplessness.

It is hard for many men to give their wives the kind of support they need. When a man is nurturing, it is usually a one-shot attempt, and if they feel awkward or clumsy, they give up and don't try again.

If a man is trying to be strong to comfort his wife, he may block his own emotions. Yet he often struggles with feelings about failing in his role as protector of the family or problem solver who "fixes" things. If he has been brought up to feel self-sufficient, he will have trouble admitting that he needs help.

A woman may misunderstand her husband's stoic ways, his refusal to talk about the child, his eagerness to return to work and normalcy. She is more likely to express her grief through crying and talking, and she thinks that if he isn't doing the same that he's not feeling pain. Men and women grieve differently.

Both need to understand and be patient with each other and encourage each other to get their feelings out in their own way, in their own time.

What both parents need is not one attempt, but a sustained effort at just being available for each other. Listen without judging. Touching, hugging, and showing signs of kindness are easy ways to be supportive and nurturing, and they can be so meaningful. Don't worry about trying to say or do the "right thing." Just be there, listen, cry and hold each other.

Ted, sixteen, broke his neck in a high school football game and died immediately. He was the youngest child in the family. His mother went into shock and depression and refused to talk to anyone. She wouldn't leave her home. She sat for hours at a time and just stared at the walls. Ted's father began to drink heavily to try to blot out his pain, both for the loss of his son and the frustration and confusion he felt over his wife's behavior. The mother blamed her husband for the accident because he had encouraged, even pushed, the boy to play football.

Within eight months after the death of the son, the couple got a divorce, a double loss for both of them. Instead of being supportive to each other in their loss, they lost each other.

The number of couples who divorce after a child dies is shockingly high: some say over seventy percent of marriages end within two years after a child dies. I believe with professional help – individual, marriage and bereavement counseling – many of these marriages could be saved.

Families as a unit have coping styles, and each family member has a unique method of coping and mourning. When any change affects the family, these coping mechanisms come into play. Coping styles are patterns of behavior that are triggered internally and acted out externally.

Seeds of how the family system handles crisis are already established in most families before a major life event like a death happens. Some families pull closer together; some divide and go their separate ways temporarily. In other families, one individual may undermine the other members' sense of reality and deny any experience of an event that is different from his or her own.

For example, a father may blame the driver of an automobile in which his daughter is killed. He may develop an abnormal hatred of that person and displace his grief at the loss of his child. When others in the family encourage him to allow his feelings of sadness and loss to surface, he may become very angry and say something like, "If John hadn't been drinking, Jennie would be alive now. It's all his fault." His wife may say tearfully, "I miss Jennie so much; she is constantly on my mind." In this case, neither person is responding to the grieving process of the other.

This is crazy-making behavior, and it can be very divisive and destructive.

In Jennie's family, the death of their daughter was the final crisis event that brought to light negative patterns of interacting that had gone on for years. If family members recognize that each is trying to cope with grief, they can be more helpful and comforting to each other.

For single parents, support can be found from friends and relatives. Don't hesitate to ask those close to you to listen to you tell the story of the death and to respect your feelings.

Grandparents will feel a tremendous surge of pain at two levels: first, for the loss of the child, and second, at seeing their own children so badly hurt, while feeling helpless to make the grief better. Permitting grandparents a role in helping with ordinary errands and household chores will help in their healing.

Other Children Suffer Too

Don't forget the needs of the surviving children in the family. They will suffer from the death of a brother or sister. Subconsciously, they may feel responsible. They will have fears about their own death.

Reactions vary, of course, from child to child, but will follow each child's predictable pattern of adjusting to stress and change. Some children will have sleeping problems, such as waking at unusual hours and having nightmares. Some may begin wetting the bed, or resume thumb sucking. Others may begin to act out in ways that get them attention, if not the reassurances of love from their parents that they crave, by misbehaving at school or home.

Paul and Jeff, twelve and thirteen-year-old brothers, were playing near a river when Jeff slipped and fell into the ice cold water and drowned. Paul had been an excellent student and an outstanding baseball player before the accident. Jeff, a year older, was the spontaneous, risk-taking one.

After the accident, Paul became restless, did poorly in school, wore dirty clothes, quit baseball and generally lost interest in life. He would go and sit by Jeff's grave for hours. The parents were in such distress themselves for about six months that they didn't realize how much trouble Paul was having. Finally, they tried counseling through the school, and that helped some. Eventually, the family moved to another town. The new location didn't have all of the old reminders of Jeff, and soon Paul began to do well in school again. Eventually, he was able to let go of the terrible guilt he carried about not being able to prevent his brother's death.

Children are easily overlooked when a family is in mourning. But they must also mourn in order to continue to live their own lives in a healthy way. They need added support, love, reassurance, and a chance to talk about their feelings, including negative ones, toward the dead sibling. Children who don't express these thoughts may carry unresolved death anxieties into adult life. If fears get shoved inside and buried in the subconscious, they will emerge and haunt the child in later life.

Small children, under seven years old, deal with grief through playing. They don't have the capacity or verbal skills to talk about their feelings. They may have overwhelming curiosity about the details of the burial, such as wondering why Jody is being put in the ground or if heaven is in the sky. These questions are the child's way of learning to his own satisfaction what this business of dying means.

A child may feel guilty for fighting with his sister; may wonder if he is going to die soon too; may be preoccupied with his sibling's toys or clothing. These behaviors are appropriate to his age and ability to understand. Adults must reassure their children in whatever way asked that they are still loved and is safe, and aren't responsible for their sibling's death. If the child seems to be stuck, and regresses into previous childish behaviors, you may want to take him or her to a child therapist or look for a support group.

You Know You're Making Progress When . . .

You can remember your child with a smile ...

You can realize the painful comments others make are made in ignorance ...

You can reach out to help someone else ...

You stop dreading holidays ...

You can sit through a church service without crying ...

You can concentrate on something besides your child ...

You can find something to thank God for ...

You can be alone in your house without it bothering you ...

You no longer feel you have to go to the cemetery every day or every week ...

You can tolerate the sound of a baby crying ...

You don't have to turn off the radio when his/her favorite music comes on ...

You can find something to laugh about ...

You can drive by the hospital or that intersection without screaming ...

You no longer feel exhausted all the time ...

You can appreciate a sunset, the smell of newly mowed grass, the pattern on a butterfly's wings

                          -- ABereaved Parent, Carmel, Indiana

CHAPTER SEVEN

LOSS AT BIRTH

Although you haven't had a chance to bond to a child lost through miscarriage, stillbirth, or in other ways at the beginning of life, there is still grief involved, which is sometimes worsened by hopes, expectations, and plans for the new baby.

When a physically defective or mentally retarded child is born, there is a sense of loss and pain in realizing that the child will never live a full life. Parents must contemplate the extra demands that care of such a child will mean. Some are able to accept the responsibility with love; others realize they don't have the emotional resources to care for such a child. The conflicts of grieving may continue for years, unless parents work through their emotions to resolution.

Miscarriages

In medical language, all miscarriages are called abortions, whether the pregnancy is terminated deliberately or by a natural process. To abort means to shorten, to remain undeveloped. The primary difference between a miscarriage and what we call an abortion is that a miscarriage is not desired by the pregnant woman, and is generally caused by some physical problem. An abortion, on the other hand, is a surgical or chemical intervention to interrupt and end the pregnancy, and is usually desired by the woman, who often did not intend to get pregnant. Both cases involve psychological pain, distress and grief.

After five years of trying every drug and technique, Sally was delighted when she finally became pregnant. The pregnancy was fine until the fourth month, when she started spotting and having cramps. A few weeks later, the doctor told her that the baby was dead inside her and that she would probably begin to abort the fetus soon. At first Sally refused to believe the doctor. She had already bought diapers and baby clothes. Slowly, as time went on and she realized that she did not feel the baby move in her womb, she accepted the fact of the death.

Finally, after two months of waiting and no sign of natural abortion, the doctor decided to do a surgical abortion. Sally almost died during this simple procedure. She hemorrhaged and had to be given several pints of blood. In a few days she went home full of someone else's blood and without a baby. Sally's grief was tremendous because she thought that this would be her only chance to have a baby. She held onto it physically and emotionally as long as possible. Eventually, she worked through her feelings, and a year or so later she was pregnant again.

While Sally's ordeal was more complex than the typical

miscarriage, the loss of an expected child can be cruelly disappointing for both parents. It may be especially hard for the woman because it is her body and she must make the physical adjustment from pregnancy to non-pregnancy and non-motherhood. Psychologically, she may feel like a failure.

In some cases, there may be feelings of relief, especially if the pregnancy was untimely. But, having adjusted to expecting a baby and anticipating the birth, it's a shock and a loss when suddenly there is no baby. It may not be a long-term adjustment, but it is painful for a while.

One woman told me that the worst part was explaining her situation to well-meaning people who kept asking her if she still had morning sickness. It was difficult for her to go through the whole story again and again. She resented the invasion of her privacy. The best way to handle such questions is to tell people simply and honestly that you have had a miscarriage. And if they pry, say that you don't want to discuss the details because it is painful for you.

Stillbirth and SIDS

Women who deliver a baby that is dead, or that dies immediately after birth, may be plagued with questions about burial, naming the child and what to tell friends. They may feel guilt, as if they did something wrong that caused the death.

Especially when the birth was carefully planned, the absence of a living baby is devastating.

There are many symptoms and emotions of grieving.

Parents report that they often wonder months or years later if the experience was real. Friends may seem to think the episode should be forgotten quickly.

Parents need to work through their grief patiently before making decisions about another pregnancy.

The death of a baby is a major loss, no matter when the death occurs, but losing an apparently healthy infant, one with whom parents have already bonded, can be especially devastating.

Sudden Infant Death Syndrome (SIDS), or crib death, is particularly baffling. An apparently healthy baby is found dead in its bed.

SIDS is the major cause of death in infants after the first week of life, and it affects about two of every 1,000 live births. Physicians don't fully understand the causes or have any means of preventing or predicting its occurrence.

Parents inevitably feel responsible for a SIDS death, although there is no reason to take such blame; SIDS is probably caused by subtle defects that doctors don't know how to identify. It is a devastating and tragic loss for parents.

The National Sudden Infant Death Syndrome Foundation in Landover, Maryland, has information that may help families grieving for this type of death. (See Appendix B.)

Abortion

Abortion differs, of course, from a miscarriage in that it requires a conscious decision on the part of the woman to terminate a pregnancy. Few women take such a decision lightly. I have seen many women struggle with the conflict of an unwanted pregnancy and the decision of whether to end a potential life. Even if a woman decides an abortion is best, she may still grieve as she would for a dying child. Much of the grieving is done before the abortion, during the decision-making process. Afterwards, for a few days, weeks, or months, it is not unusual for the woman to experience some sadness when thinking about the abortion. Again, she must work through all her feelings or the loss may haunt her forever.

The hardest part is making the decision to have an abortion in the first place. Generally, such a decision is tied to conflict. If you are pressured to get the abortion against your wishes because of threats by the father ("If you have the kid I will have nothing to do with you"), bribery ("I'll pay for it, dear"), or through shame ("What will the neighbors say?"), you may have a much more difficult time processing the grief later. The final choice must be made by the woman herself. No amount of coercion for or against the abortion by parents, lover, husband or friends will lead to the "right" decision for you.

All of the stages of grief will be there. A woman who learns she is unintentionally pregnant will first react with denial and disbelief. The first part of the grief cycle is a wish that "it isn't true," "not now," "not me." Your second reaction will probably be anger – often at the father, for not accepting some responsibility for birth control or for being sexually demanding at the wrong time. You may also be angry at yourself for the same reasons. The constant worry about an unwanted pregnancy will overshadow everything in your life at this time.

The next stage will be bargaining. You may wish for some "natural" event to occur that will end the pregnancy so you won't have to decide. Or you may try to make a "deal" with God to never do anything wrong for the rest of your life if only He will make the pregnancy go away, or give you a "sign" that you should have the baby, or in some way help you to get out of this mess.

The fourth stage is depression, feeling low or down. At this stage you experience all your unresolved emotions, including guilt, anger, disappointment, and sadness. You have to face key conflicts. You may feel that by having an abortion you are giving up a part of yourself and a child of yours. You must deal with concerns about abandoning a potential life, or the moral issue of killing a being with a soul. During this stage there may be a lot of tears and feelings of self-pity. It's better to feel those things than to try to be stoic and keep very strong emotions inside. Take as long as you need to work through this part of the process. Stay with your sadness and your pain. In a short time you will know what the right decision is for you.

Acceptance is the final stage of grieving. If you have decided to go ahead and get the abortion, you will now be able to make the necessary arrangements and follow them through. In the early stages of the pregnancy, an abortion can usually be handled by a safe and simple procedure in a doctor's office. There is little or no physical pain. There may still be psychological pain or regrets, but if you worked through the grieving process, you will be able to reduce the time of inner conflict and get on with your life.

A woman who decides to complete an unplanned

pregnancy will be sure she has made the right decision if she knows she has weighed her choices.

Adoption

Putting an infant or child up for adoption is a difficult choice that some women face. And it is a loss that creates grief.

Consider Maggie. She found herself pregnant with her lover's child. She was thirty-eight at the time, divorced with two teen-aged daughters. She didn't want to have an abortion, but she also didn't want to raise another child. So she talked the situation over with her lover. He agreed to support her during the pregnancy and to pay for the delivery of the baby, provided that she put the infant up for adoption.

She agreed, and she saw the baby only in the viewing room. Maggie released him with love to begin life with his new parents. Now she sometimes misses him, because she had always wanted a son. She thinks of him sometimes and wonders what he looks like and how he is doing in school. But she has few regrets about her decision.

Maggie was mature enough to make a rational decision. But many women in similar circumstances are not. Becoming pregnant is a major event in a woman's life, and giving up a child is like letting go of an important part of her. With a growing number of teen-age pregnancies, the problem is a frequent one, and it is always difficult for the individuals involved. It is an increasing dilemma for society.

Along with sexual activity must go the ability to respond to the risk of pregnancy. That's what responsibility is: the ability to respond. The responsibility for pregnancy belongs to both partners in any sexual relationship.

Traditionally, women have been the ones to pay the price of an unplanned pregnancy. But it takes two people, male and female, to create a child or a pregnancy, and both of these people should share equal responsibility for either the prevention of the pregnancy or for the creation of new life. One of the things a man can do is ask a woman if she might become pregnant if they have sex. If she's not using any birth control measures, then they should refrain, or he should use a condom or other contraceptive.

Still, there are times when precautions fail and an unwanted pregnancy occurs. Mark learned after his high school graduation that Sue, whom he had slept with once, was pregnant. Mark had asked Sue if she was using a method of birth control, and she said she was on the "pill." She was on the "pill," but had taken it only for a few days and it was not yet effective.

Both young people agonized over their dilemma. They did not really love each other. Mark planned to go to college and could not afford to support a wife and child. They talked over the options, including abortion, with her parents and his mother. Finally, Sue decided to have the child on her own. Her parents stood by her, and Mark checked with her often, even though he lived in another city. She worked and earned enough money to pay for her pre-natal care and delivery. A few years after her son was born, she fell in love and married, and her husband adopted her little boy.

Only a few years ago, this story would have had another ending. The couple would have been forced to marry;

another marriage would have been based on a short-term spontaneous sexual encounter, and would most likely have developed into a relationship built on resentment and anger rather than on mutual love and respect.

In the process of deciding what to do about the pregnancy, all parties were able to think about future consequences, evaluate the various courses of action, and come to terms with their feelings of grief and loss created by the situation. Sue chose to not let Mark see the baby after he was born. Recently, Mark told me that every time he sees a cute, blond three-year-old, he feels a sense of longing and regret at not being able to see his son and be involved in his life. Mark's mother says that she, too, feels sad that she is not able to be a grandparent to the child.

Though the aftermath was difficult for all parties, the decision had to be the mother's. Others must take comfort in knowing that the best thing was done for the mother and child. People closely involved in an unplanned pregnancy feel many of the emotions of grief when they lose contact with the child. They must – as with a death – let themselves feel the pain, then let it go, and move on into the future.

Many situations in life involve loss and are difficult and painful, but they can also be wonderful opportunities to grow and to develop sensitivity about our future encounters and to have more empathy for others. We do not always get what we think we want in life, and maybe it is a blessing in disguise.

Where you used to be, there is a hole in the world, which I find myself constantly walking around in the daytime, and falling in at night. I miss you like hell.
-Edna St. Vincent Millay

Unable are the loved to die. For love is immortality.
-Emily Dickinson

Death leaves a heartache no one can heal, love leaves a memory no one can steal.

-From a headstone in Ireland

CHAPTER EIGHT

DEATH OF FRIENDS AND SIBLINGS

Death of Friends

When a close friend dies, especially if the person is about your same age and the same sex as you, it often forces you to consider your own death. The effect can be startling. The death of a friend is often a milestone event – an occurrence that leads to rethinking and possibly rearranging personal priorities. Because we may identify so strongly with a close friend, that person's death brings up reminders of our mortality more than the death of a parent, child or spouse may do.

The more you have in common with the friend, the more his death will make you contemplate and wonder about your own. Sometimes a surviving friend will realize, "It could just as easily have been me." Such a death has a way of reminding us how vulnerable we are, how fragile life sometimes is. And it may cause you to reassess the direction your own life has been taking.

109

Jack's story is a good example. A successful stock market broker, Jack made a lot of money but didn't spend as much time with his family as he wanted. His job was demanding and required him to work long hours. But about three years ago, one of his best friends, a man who worked in the same office, had a heart attack. He died while celebrating his twin daughters' eighteenth birthday in a restaurant. The man was fifty-one years old. Jack was thirty-nine at the time.

Not long after his friend's death, Jack started to have chest pains during stressful business meetings. Finally, he had a good physical check-up, including an electrocardiogram. He received a clean bill of health. But the chest pains continued. He kept thinking of the death of his friend. Jack thought about how much his friend missed in life by not watching his children develop into adults. He saw how tough it was for his friend's widow to manage for the first year or so.

Jack realized that these concerns were projections of worries about his own death. He didn't want his life to end the way his friend's had. He talked his feelings over with his wife and children, and decided to quit his job and change his lifestyle. The family moved to a smaller town, bought an older house and remodeled it as a family project. Jack is now the proprietor of a small art gallery. He is relaxed, has gotten acquainted with his children, and says that he has never been so happy in his life. And he has had no more chest pains.

The impact of a death of someone outside the immediate family will depend on several factors, including the length of the relationship, the intensity of the relationship, the circumstances of the death, the age of the survivor, the survivor's prior experiences with death, and the emotional connection between the survivor and the deceased.

Though most people understand that someone who loses a family member grieves, fewer people realize the special circumstances and trauma that one goes through when an intimate friend becomes ill or has a fatal disease or accident.

When I was in the fourth grade, we lived in a small farming community in Michigan. There were a few Mexican families who lived in a small barrio there; they were laborers who picked sugar beets. One child from the barrio, Maria, and I would stay on the playground long after school was over and she would teach me Spanish. She was polite and bright and shy. Our friendship flourished and within a few months we had become best friends.

I remember the shock and sadness I felt the day I went to school and was told that Maria had been hit by a car the afternoon before, sometime around five o'clock, as she walked home after our Spanish lesson. Our class visited the funeral home. I felt a profound sense of loss. Afterwards, I remembered the words that she taught me. I paid a lot more attention to cars when I crossed the street after that. And I have always had a special place in my heart for Mexicans.

Death of Lovers

When someone's lover dies, there is not always a place for the aggrieved survivor to turn for comfort, especially if the lover was married or the two were of the same sex. Neither extramarital affairs nor homosexual relationships are usually sanctioned by society, and many people – sometimes even close friends and relatives – fail to realize the sympathy that the survivor of such a loss needs.

Marriage is still the predominantly accepted bond between adults. And most other relationships are formed within social institutions such as the family, school, church, neighborhood or work place. People who live outside the prevailing social norms are frequently penalized by discrimination, non-acceptance, fear, rejection and hostility. Often the "illicit" relationship is kept secret, and many acquaintances may not realize what a loss someone has suffered if they're not aware of the person's intimate connection to someone who has recently died.

It is difficult to assess the number of people who are affected by such situations. But I would guess that the number is much higher than most people imagine; possibly twenty percent of the population fits into one category or the other at some time in their lives. Because of the negative attitudes that prevail in society, most people are reluctant to take the risk of openly revealing same-sex or extramarital intimate relationships. Since discretion is the predominant behavior pattern in such a relationship, the person involved is often without a support system when a deep loss occurs.

A former student came to class extremely distraught one night. Let's call her Lynn. Her married lover in a seven-year relationship had just had a stroke and was in the hospital. He couldn't talk and was very ill. Lynn got the news from neighbors in his apartment building. When she called the hospital to see how he was, she had to lie about her relationship to him, saying that she was his sister. She got sketchy news of his condition, and found out that his wife and daughter were keeping a constant vigil. Lynn wanted to go to him, and she knew that he would want her there. Yet if she went and created a scene, it would be worse for everyone. Lynn was so worried about her lover and so full of conflict about her options. She felt shut *out* of his life.

He recovered for a short time, and went home to live with his wife for three months before his second and final stroke. During that time, Lynn's life was a nightmare. She was beside herself with yearning to be with him and consumed by fears about his health. She never had a chance to talk to him again. She saw the notice of his death in the obituary column of the newspaper. When Lynn went to the funeral, she sat in the back row, a widow without support, suffering her loss in solitude, crying her tears alone.

Lesbians and gay men suffer the same lack of support from society at large. In the past decade or so, gays have received more understanding and acceptance through some political and educational activism and because of more media exposure. Yet our society still discriminates against homosexuals.

This results in little or no support from the usual places — family, friends, and fellow workers — when one partner dies, particularly if the relationship is still "in the closet."

Many gay people, especially older ones, have not revealed their sexual preference to relatives, neighbors, fellow workers, and others. Most gay couples, however, have a circle of trusted friends and these friends become the caring support system. People are people, and when someone you love dies or is injured or stricken by a fatal disease, the fear of losing the lover is very painful emotionally. It is helpful to have acknowledgment and support from the people in your social environment, but grieving is a solitary experience, and you will do your own grieving in your personal, unique way, with or without the support of others.

Death of Siblings

The death of a brother or sister is usually a major loss, although several factors need to be considered. The ages of the siblings, the closeness of the relationship, and the resolution of sibling rivalry are some important considerations.

Brothers and sisters have the potential for the longest ongoing relationships in the human life span. When young children suffer the loss of a sister or brother, it is often a confusing mystery. Sometimes they feel guilty that they caused the death because they wished for the death or for the other to "go away forever" in a moment of anger. Or they may feel that they could have done something heroic to save the life of the other – or, in the case of an accident, that they should have died instead of the one who did.

It's important to explore these feelings with children and allow them to express both negative and positive feelings toward their deceased brother or sister.

When adult siblings die, the emotional impact is usually reduced. Often their lives have taken them in different directions, and the intensity of early childhood connections has begun to fade. However, there is often a profound feeling of sadness and sorrow, like losing some part of yourself. It is losing a part of your past, of common experiences and parents and places.

There is, of course, a difference if you are close by during a long period of illness and gradual deterioration. You will feel the impact of the death more than if you have had a long separation by years and/or distance.

Adult siblings often find they are very different from each other in interests, values and personalities. If there are conflicts between you that were not cleared up before the death, you may experience guilt or regret or other unresolved feelings. But the connecting bonds of your parents and childhood experiences remain. In other cases, brothers and sisters will again live together or close to each other after their families have been raised. The main effect of a sibling's death is to remind you of your own vulnerability or aging, and what a fragile gift your own life is.

Death of Others

We also grieve over the deaths of people who are not our immediate family, friends, or lovers. A former teacher, minister, or mentor may die, and even if you have not been in contact with this person for years, you may feel deep sadness and loss.

There are times when an entire country will be in mourning, as when the head of state is assassinated. For example, the world reeled when President John Kennedy was killed. The shock and horror of his assassination threw the United States into mass mourning. Almost every American old enough to remember 1963 can recall what he or she was doing on that fateful day.

The murder of musician John Lennon in 1980 also touched off a worldwide outpouring of grief. As the most creative member of the Beatles, a revolutionary group of musicians, he had expressed the feelings of millions of young people for twenty years. People all over the world strongly identified with him, and when he was assassinated during a time of renewed personal creativity in his life, thousands of young people and adults felt the loss very deeply.

To some people, the death of an admired mentor or culturally important person may be more affecting than any loss they have experienced of members of their own families. Many times the deaths of key entertainment figures are followed by several suicides among fans. There is a fascination with deaths of folk heroes such as James Dean, Rudolph Valentino, Marilyn Monroe or Elvis Presley.

Collective grief is experienced on different levels. First are the subjective or personal feelings of loss, which vary according to how strongly you felt about the person who has just died. Secondly, you come face to face with your own vulnerability and the fact that life can be snuffed out so quickly. A third issue to confront is the potential violence that lies so close to the surface in "civilized" human beings. The political or cultural aftermath can have an impact for years.

Seeing violence across the world daily in the news or in fictionalized television shows does not really have the impact that the death of a "real" person has, even if we do not know that individual personally.

Grief is experienced collectively when several people share similar feelings at the same time. Anxiety and fears about how to achieve an orderly transition from the initial chaos of an assassination to new leadership prevail among those affected. They may share feelings of anger and outrage and want to get even with the killer. Because this is not possible for them as individuals, their frustrations may make them feel impotent, powerless, out of control, and paranoid, as if victimized by a psychotic or an international plot.

Rumors and paranoid fears run rampant. Such a death becomes a "media event," and it is almost impossible to carry on life in a regular way. The rituals of a state funeral or a national or international observation of mourning are necessary to allow some time for a cooling off from negative feelings. The rituals of the funeral are for the living.

Assassination attempts have a similar effect, but do not carry the same degree of impact as a death. In a shorter period, the country returns to normal and individuals resume their usual activities. But lingering fear or sadness remains for some time after the event.

The deaths of Robert Kennedy, Mahatma Gandhi, and Martin Luther King dramatize the emotional power of a public figure cut down in his prime. Through the senselessness of their untimely deaths, they may in fact have had more impact on social change than they had through their living words and actions.

Unlike life, death cannot be taken away from man, and therefore we may consider it as the gift of God.

- Seneca

CHAPTER NINE

DEATH OF SELF: THE DYING PROCESS

One of the most challenging experiences of the human condition is to come to terms with being alone. We spend most of our lives involved in one relationship after another. Most people go from living with parents to living with a spouse or lover, then to becoming parents themselves. Even those without families are usually wrapped up in friendships, work relationships, social activities or projects and other ways of connecting with people.

We continually seek and desire the company of others. As a result, we think we need others to complete us and make us whole. People often stay in destructive and unhappy relationships because at some deep level they fear being lonely or being left alone. When we relate to others, we have the illusion of being secure; we want to be taken care of and loved. We fear loneliness because we're afraid that we can't take care of ourselves and meet our own needs. Everyone experiences the anxiety of being alone to some extent.

The fear of being alone began when we were infants, when we were truly helpless and dependent on another for our very survival. So great is our need for another human being during infancy that subconsciously we continue to seek security in our relationships with other human beings as adults. And we fear losing them. We think that only through others can we avoid discomfort and relieve our fears. In extreme cases of insecurity, a person may feel worthless and think that life has no meaning and no fulfillment unless it is shared with someone else.

Loneliness is associated with feelings of losing contact, separation, isolation, and abandonment. For some, the thought of being alone conjures up feelings of anguish, despair, desolation, panic and terror – the worst possible fate.

The reality of the human condition is that we are always essentially alone. The challenge of the human condition is to come to terms with our singularity, our uniqueness. No one else can live your life. You are born alone and you die alone. No one else experiences the events in life in exactly the same way you do, not a spouse or a child or a close sibling or a best friend. Your thoughts, impressions, values and decisions are yours alone. When you are dependent on another, you've chosen that dependency as your way of life.

You may be in the same place with others or in common situations with others but you are unique. There may be people around you, but they are not you. There is the essential you that you carry through all your experiences. No one else is ever-present. We alone live in our bodies, with our thoughts and feelings.

No other experience is more private, more alone, than death. Even with loved ones around, a person slips away from the known life into the unknown alone. She cannot go back and tell others about it; she can't bring someone with her. We know when we die we won't be around to share in the lives of those we care about.

Thoughts of our own death or the death of someone we depend on for survival or companionship force us to confront our aloneness. We may face the prospect with dread and despair, or we may start to realize that we are able to take care of ourselves.

Much of the resistance to accepting death is demonstrated in our efforts to hold on and cling to others in life. When you must face the death of a loved one, or your own death, it's important to realize that being alone and loneliness are not the same thing. Being alone gives you time to think, relax, read, enjoy nature, create, meditate, pray – to appreciate and know yourself. This can enrich and give value to your life. Learning the value of being alone can help you transcend your fears, and to begin to know and love yourself.

Transcendence is the ability to overcome the primitive fears that we all experience in life, including the fear of being alone. Opportunities to rise above these fears are presented to us occasionally throughout our lives, whenever major life events related to loss, change and death occur. If we are ready, these experiences can be catalysts: opportunities to move beyond our old patterns of being, and to find inner strength and resources we didn't know we had.

Denial and Hope

It takes courage to face our basic raw emotions, to allow anguish and despair to surface, to confront the sources of our resistances. Yet if we do confront these fears, our own death will be easier.

Most people die the way they lived. If a person has had a pattern of ignoring unpleasant experiences, pretending they never happened, she will handle news of encroaching death the same way. If a person has been explosive and quick to display anger, then he will react in a similar way to the realization of his impending death. If a person has been open and willing to talk about feelings, most likely he or she will handle the dying process the same way.

What is your process? How do you react to bad news, to extreme stress, to change, to disappointment and loss?

Our patterns of reacting to critical life events are established very early in life, possibly even at birth, and if these patterns are not raised to a conscious level and altered, they will remain essentially the same. These patterns are called defense mechanisms or coping styles. They include psychological techniques that protect people from emotional danger. Sometimes they are effective and sometimes not. Some examples of coping styles are denial, intellectualizing, acting-out, projection, displacement, fantasy, repression, dissociation, hypochondriacal behavior, humor and delusions.

The age of the person who is dying has a significant effect on the coping style. For example, young children have not developed the ability to intellectualize, or to use humor, and older people are not rewarded for childish acting-out behavior.

Individual attitudes toward life and death change over the years, which affects the way an individual will handle the news of his or her death.

Denial is the first part of the process of dealing with the idea of dying. Death is such a big concept that it is hard to adjust to it all at once. Typically, when someone is ill, he has a chance to adjust to a series of smaller losses such as surgery, losing hair with chemotherapy, feeling weaker, incomplete recovery, relapse and returning to the hospital after a time at home. Each time a loss like this occurs, denial is reduced and hope is altered. Denial and hope are partners that keep a dying person going – alive and experiencing feelings – and allow him time to adjust.

Denial of the reality of one's death protects the psyche from the harshness and pain of giving up life. Hope lets us endure and continue to have a meaningful future, even if the future is shortened. Hope is sustaining. It carries you over, and bridges the gap between finding out about your death and accepting it. Hope is the bright light during a time of ambiguity and confusion, protest and bargaining.

You may hope for a scientific breakthrough, a new and complete cure. There may be hope for the tests and the medical reports to be wrong, or to belong to someone else. Sometimes these thoughts are called false hope. They may not be realistic; in fact, they may be a form of repression, but they buy time to adjust to the idea of dying.

Because we all have plans and goals, it takes readjustment

to alter or surrender the future. Gradually, as reality takes over more and more, the achievable goals are realized and the impossible goals are given up or changed to ones that can be completed in the time left.

Sometimes having goals keeps us going. As the ragtime pianist and composer Eubie Blake entered his final decade of life, he received adulation and attention that he had not experienced earlier in his life. Still vigorous in his nineties, he seemed to set living to be one hundred as his goal. His health declined in the last few years, but he reached one hundred, and fans celebrated with concerts and the press covered his birthday. Blake died five days later.

Denial, hope, and acceptance are frequently present at the same time, in varying degrees, during the initial phases of coming to terms with one's death.

Consider Edna, a mother of three small children. She found out that she had terminal cancer when she was thirty-two years old. When she called me from the hospital to tell me the diagnosis, she didn't seem too concerned. She talked of new drugs and other hopeful treatments. Edna was a nurse and knew that the usual survival time was about six months, but *emotionally* she was not ready to accept the facts. She had to work out her internal conflicts.

In the beginning, Edna was in despair about her plans for her children, fussy about their daily habits, clothes, and behavior. At the end, she hardly knew when they were around. She did die within six months. She changed her goals. She settled for being involved in one more birthday instead of a whole lifetime with them. When the birthday (hers) was celebrated, she let go. She accepted her plight, her death. She realized that she must let go of her family and conserve what little energy she had just to survive another day.

For Edna, hope was transformed from clinging and clutching at life to accepting her own end. The night that she died, I was keeping vigil so that her husband could get some rest. She was terribly thin, and she had tumors all over her body. Before her husband left the hospital that evening, she asked me to help her put on some make-up. She said she wanted to look pretty for him because he had been so good to her while she was sick. She died with her make-up on. Hope? Or acceptance? Or reality?

Many who are dying withdraw more and more from involvement in the affairs of everyday life. Hope becomes transformed into faith. We can define hope as desire accompanied by expectation through anticipation, while faith is complete trust and confidence. These two can merge in the final stage of dying for those who have faith that life will go on, that there is life after death or that death is somehow right. As the plans and goals of day-to-day living are shed, expectations change to looking forward to death – to the release from physical pain, withdrawal from the pressures of life.

Self-Awareness

Our understanding of death as a concept changes over the course of our life. Understanding is an intellectual process. It reaches deeper levels of consciousness according to our level of awareness, beliefs, experiences, and feelings of sympathy.

Feelings about death involve emotions such as love, hate, anger, joy and fear. Emotions such as fear are part of our basic survival instinct and serve as warning signs of danger. The fight-or-flight response in animals is part of the alarm system we humans carry with us. If you step out into the street in front of traffic, your body will startle you with a shot of adrenaline, and you will react by jumping to safety. Other emotions, such as joy and love, are connected with empathy, the participation or sharing in the feelings of another.

We all operate our lives from both places – intellect and emotion – but not necessarily in balance. One or the other is usually predominant. Most of the time we are thinking, rational, and predictable in our behavior. Yet if we do not allow the emotional side of ourselves expression, feelings will pile up and often explode in anger, hostility, or violence. Some people hold it all inside and implode, explode inwardly and get sick physically.

Many adults are afraid of and confused by our emotions. We were taught from infancy to control ourselves. Control messages take many forms: don't get angry; big boys don't cry; nice girls are reserved and quiet; don't act like a tomboy. We learn to deny the feeling side of ourselves at an early age. We are embarrassed if we lose control. The motto of western society is BE STOIC! HOLD IT IN! STAY IN CONTROL! DON'T BE EMOTIONAL!

If we cry or act angry, joyful, or happy we are not sure how others will respond. One reason adults lose the ability to be playful and have fun is that we were taught to deny emotional expression. Emotions, in fact, are neither good nor bad. They just are. They are part of all of us. Some are pleasant and some are unpleasant. The emotional part of grieving and mourning is prolonged and more difficult for people who learned to be stoic, who cut themselves off from their feelings.

You can learn to recognize your emotions. Here's one way. Any time that you feel a strong negative reaction to a person, place or thing, your emotional side is giving you a clue that you have some unresolved issues that need attention. If you stop and take the time to analyze what happened, to recognize and identify your feelings, you will be able to begin to resolve that particular problem for yourself.

It's rewarding to reclaim and make friends with the emotional side of yourself. Do not deny and be afraid of your emotions; acknowledge and respect them. They are an important part of you. Accepting our feelings as well as our intellect helps us to be balanced human beings.

As we integrate our emotions with our intellect, we become more self-aware, more self-conscious. It is like turning on a light using a rheostat, a switch that gradually regulates the brightness or dimness of an electric light. The older we are, the more time and experiences we have had. Time gives us the potential to be advanced in awareness, and gradually our light can shine brighter, so that by old age we will have accepted death as the next and final uncompleted task in life. Learning from life and being attuned to our reactions are how we achieve self-awareness, enlightenment.

Age at Death

An infant or mentally disabled person has a very dim light, very little self-awareness. Knowledge of or emotional attachment to their lives is minimal or non-existent.

A pre-school child imagines death primarily as a separation from her parents. She fears losing them, and she fears going to a hospital. These fears are more real than the fear of death. With some explanation, she may come to think of death as being like a long sleep or going to see God – whom she imagines as an extension of her parents, an authority figure.

Between the ages of six and twelve, death is still a fantasy, distant and unreal. If a child this age has been told he will die, he may misbehave or complain of every little ache and pain to get attention and the reassurance that he is loved and won't be abandoned. The child has become involved with people outside the family, but hasn't much concept of the future. Death may be seen as an interruption of achievements – "But I've just learned to ride my bike!" – or a disruption of friendships.

These children should continue with normal activities like school, sports and hobbies, and with friendships as long as possible. Those are the important aspects of life for this age group.

In adolescence, there's a growing sense of identity and the uniqueness of "me" as an individual. A teenager who is dying may feel that knowing she is valuable, has a special identity and worth, is the most important feeling to embrace.

Adolescents still don't have a sense of what it means to live for a long time, even though they're beginning to plan for the future. That's why young people make the best soldiers: they're strong, daring, willing to risk their lives for glory and adventure and recognition.

This is the time of life when a peer group is important. Adolescents care about what their friends think of them. Physical image is also important, and the bodily changes that result from illness may be especially difficult at this age.

The adolescent facing death should stay in touch with friends as much as possible. Acceptance and love from his peers, and social status, may be more important to him than his parents. The adolescent's tendency to veer wildly from mature self-sufficiency to childlike vulnerability will be more extreme when compounded by the stress of serious illness.

One young man, seventeen years old, was on his school's football team when he found out that he had leukemia. He practiced with the team as long as possible, played in the first game of the season, and died before the season ended. As he adjusted to the idea of his death, his biggest concern was what his friends thought of him. He worried about letting the team down. The entire football team, including the coach and cheerleaders, visited him in the hospital. They reassured him that he was important to them. He died feeling validated in the way that mattered most to him.

In early adulthood, news of fatal illness is understandably met with outrage and fury. "It isn't fair," "I'm just getting started in life," "Not me ... not now." The light of self-awareness is getting brighter, only to be snuffed out prematurely. There is so much to do and not enough time. Relationships may be fewer than in adolescence, but they are often better in quality and are more important. Family and a few special friends are the main sources of psychological support.

An adult under forty will greet death with severe feelings of disappointment, anger, and frustration. It's unfair. There is so much to *do*, because at this stage of life, we prove our worth by doing – being *involved* in politics or community groups, working, having children, going to P.T.A. or Little League meetings, traveling, learning, and achieving in our work.

Young adults must shorten goals and expectations for their life. They will have to settle for another birthday, as Edna did, or one more holiday spent with the family. The final time can be lived to the fullest, but the future is only tomorrow.

After forty, news of impending death may be somewhat more acceptable. Middle-age, roughly forty to sixty-five years, is the time of life to enjoy the benefits of the work of the previous years. Sometime during their forties, many people experience another identity crisis similar to that of adolescence, as they face changes in physical appearance, a decline in stamina, status, and possibly reduced sexual interest. Sometimes it is an opportunity to turn inward and to evaluate life's goals and work, to consider the quality of life instead of its quantity. Time perspective also changes, and people begin to think about the number of years they have left, instead of the number of years since their birth.

It is during the middle years that most people bury their parents and become the "older" generation in their families. Companionship becomes more important in relationships than sex, and new depth of sharing and understanding in marriage may result. Adjustment in the middle years may involve learning to shift from physically-based values to wisdom-based values, and finding new and creative solutions to current and future problems.

It is also the time when the nest empties. Children leave home and parents can live without the demands and pressures of raising them. In these years, there's a high incidence of divorce, but the marriages that make it through become better than ever. Men generally become more gentle and sensitive, and women become more assertive.

Many of life's tasks have been completed, yet these years are still active and productive. Death means that careers will be interrupted and loving relationships with spouses, children, grandchildren, and friends will be cut short. Death denies people of this age a chance to harvest the fruits of their labors: to develop leisure interests, to travel, to enjoy retirement and grandchildren and family.

Death now ends life before it is finished, like a thief.

Some of us are able to regard death during the middle years from a more philosophical position, thinking of the meaning of life and death, evaluating whether our life has had value to ourselves and others.

In advanced adulthood, we become aware that death is closer. In the sixties, we re-evaluate setting new goals and ways to use time. We may believe that living past sixty-five years is a bonus. Only a few decades ago, the average life span was much shorter: fifty-two for women and forty-eight for men. Now women live to seventy-two years, and men to sixty-eight years on the average. Many people live past the end of their work life.

In old age, one reviews one's life and may feel satisfied that it has been worthwhile or may try to repair former failures.

Death now is less feared, sometimes even anticipated with interest. In the case of those with poor health or a chronic illness, death may be strongly welcomed. If life has been a disappointment, then death will be less acceptable until some of the problems of one's life have been resolved.

On the other hand, old age and retirement can be the most delightful time of life, full of peace, happiness, and contentment. In such cases, though one may hate to go, death is more readily accepted as a natural part of the life cycle. Most elderly people who truly fear death have not yet made peace with themselves. When a life has been fulfilling and has had an impact on others, the light of this life can reach its peak of brightness, then flicker and, like a shooting star, streak across the sky in a final blaze of glory.

Other Fears: How You Die

For many, the fear of death is primarily about how you will die. Worries about physical deterioration and appearance, pain, panic, and dying alone or in an institution can preoccupy your thoughts and delay coming to terms with death.

A friend of mine with a severe chronic lung problem partially accepted the inevitable prospect of her death, but would panic at the thought of suffocating. She often said that she had come to terms with the fact that she was dying, but she wished it were over. Her fear was all about how she would die. She prayed for her end to come in her sleep or in a merciful coma.

Specific personal fears will be of great concern during the time when you are told the nature and extent of your illness. In the beginning, when you first acknowledged symptoms such as a tumor, pain, or unusual bleeding, you most likely also experienced a psychological fear about the nature and extent of the physical problem. Maybe all the facts were unknown and unconfirmed at that point in time. When you were told the results and probable outcome of your disease after diagnostic tests or surgery, you may have felt relief at knowing the truth. Yet feelings of numbness, shock, disbelief, great anguish, and fear might also be present at the moment of truth.

Final Decisions

The crisis of knowing that you are going to die creates a need to rearrange life plans, goals, activities, and relationships. Dealing with your own death is a new learning process, perhaps the most important one so far. You are forced to re-evaluate and re-learn something important: how to live and how to die.

At first, the news will elicit feelings of anger, fear, doubt, dread, insecurity, confusion, rage, disappointment and many other feelings. After a while, your old barriers and defenses will crumble. Then you will begin to talk and make decisions that will affect you and your loved ones who will survive your death.

Deciding on the disposal of your body after death can be difficult. Burial or cremation may seem dismal or unthinkable prospects. The thought of an autopsy, or donating useful organs to other people, may be morbid and painful. These concerns may be partly related to the denial of your death, and partly related to the fear of non-being.

After physical death our bodies quickly begin to break down, just as any organic matter does. We no longer can experience sensations. Thus, when we think about the choices of burial or cremation, and choose "none of the above," we are projecting fears and feelings onto our bodies past their usefulness to us.

The sooner these issues are worked through and resolved, the better. You may choose to ignore or avoid making decisions about your burial for yourself, but open and frank discussion of your wishes with your next of kin or closest friends will do a great deal to relieve everyone of these worries.

Dealing with the knowledge of your impending death involves facing the fears of letting go of life as you have known it and lived it so far. It is time to make decisions, to resolve problems, to make amends, and to clean up outstanding issues in relationships. This gift of time between knowing about your death and when you actually die may be used in a beneficial way for yourself and for others: it is a chance to complete your financial affairs, resolve unfinished conflicts, and say goodbye with love.

The only way to prepare for sudden, accidental or unexpected death is to realize that we are all vulnerable to death. Make a will; discuss burial plans and financial issues with your family. Regularly keep them informed about changes in life insurance benefits, pensions and keys to your safe deposit box.

A loved one's death is a difficult enough crisis to survive without having to cope with such problems.

Settle important issues as rapidly as you can – financial affairs that affect those who survive you, problems in relationships, and questions about your life's priorities. You can't be guaranteed a future, since no one can be fully protected against death or tragedy. But having the loose ends of your life tied up as much as possible makes today, as well as tomorrow, more peaceful and fulfilling.

Relative Positions of Loss to Self

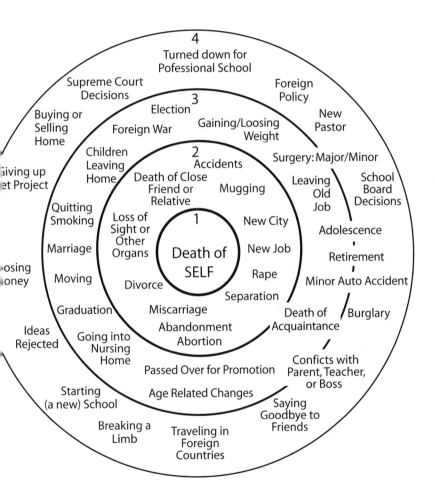

Figure 2

RICHARD CORY

Whenever Richard Cory went down town
   We people on the pavement looked at him;
He was a gentleman from sole to crown,
   Clean favored, and imperially slim.

And he was always quietly arrayed,
   And he was always human when he talked;
But still he fluttered pulses when he said,
   "Good-morning," and he glittered when he walked.

And he was rich – yes, richer than a king –
   And admirably schooled in every grace:
In fine, we thought that he was everything
   To make us wish that we were in his place.

So on we worked, and waited for the light,
   And went without the meat, and cursed the bread;
And Richard Cory, one calm summer night,
   Went home and put a bullet through his head.

- Edwin Arlington Robinson

CHAPTER TEN

DEATH BY SUICIDE

Martha wept as she told about her son, John. He visited her a week before he hanged himself. The night before he was to return to his city, he put his arm around his mother and told her that he loved her, and that she had been a good mother to him. All of this was unusual, she said, because he had never been demonstrative before. She thought that he was changing for the better. Earlier in the day he had commented jokingly that he wouldn't be around to enjoy a family party planned for two weeks later. His mother took that to mean that he would be back at his home. After his death, she was able to piece together the hidden meaning in what he had been saying.

What bothered her most was that John had left a will disposing of all his property, his apartment was immaculate, he had on his best clothes, and he had written out checks to all his creditors. On the checks to the utility companies, he had filled in their names, put "FINAL BILL," and left the amount blank.

His mother said that John was quiet and unassuming, never any trouble to anyone ... a loner. He was the same way in death. How consistent we are.

Psychologically, this twenty-five-year-old young man is almost a classic case. He lived by himself in a city away from his only support system, his family, and had not developed any other ties. He lived in San Francisco, the city with the highest suicide rate in the country. He had completed a bachelor's degree in college, and had a good technical job with a national company. He had a new car, a nice apartment, and plenty of money. He had achieved all that life held for him, but he was still not fulfilled or happy. He was empty. The American Dream had failed him – or he had failed it. He had it all, and yet he had nothing. He was white, male and single – all high risk factors for suicide. He had no friends.

The lack of contact with other human beings was probably the single most critical factor in his suicide. Successes in life are often meaningless if they are not shared with others. His lifetime pattern of extreme introversion indicated a prevailing feeling of worthlessness and insecurity in relationships. Perhaps the few times he tried to reach out to others in his life for friendship, he was rebuffed and so learned to give up too easily, only to feel more isolated and without value. Possibly the problem was that he simply lacked social skills. Yet he expected to be rejected and created situations where this would happen. His worthlessness kept being validated.

What was there to live for? He had few memories of past happiness and satisfaction, even though he did the things that are supposed to make people happy. He had an education, a good job, and the material accoutrements to signal to others that he was successful. With no satisfaction in the present, the feelings of emptiness continued. For someone like John, the loneliness continues, if there are no friends. No one cares if you live or die. No one to miss you; no one to grieve. No difference in the world, with or without you.

And finally, he had no *hope*. No hope of anything different, no expectation of satisfaction in the future.

With no ties to the past, no present, and no future, there was no reason to live.

John was a bright young man. He made his decision based on the available evidence. And in the post-decision euphoria, he cleaned up his life. He said his goodbyes, gave away his possessions, and paid his bills. "He was never any trouble to anybody," his mother told me. But she was wrong. And he was wrong to feel that no one cared. Now his mother cries, and his father can't; they wonder what went wrong.

Guilt and Regrets

The word "survive" comes from two Latin words: super, which means over, and vivere, which means to live. If someone you have loved and been involved with commits suicide, he or she has left you behind to survive. As a survivor you must, then, go on and start over to live again.

If the suicide came as a shock and surprise, your grieving process will be doubly difficult. Probably the most powerful and hostile rejection a person can make of another is to commit suicide. To the survivor, the death seems like a photograph, a flat, two-dimensional image of an incident. Many people can look at the image and relate to parts of it, but no one person can know or understand all dimensions of the event totally. During the grieving process, it is necessary to come to terms with the past issues, stresses, and problems remaining from the relationship with the suicidee. Because there are always so many questions left unanswered, this can be a very difficult and painful experience.

Every person who has been involved with the suicidee will be forced to examine himself for his part in the death, and all may feel some guilt, responsibility, and self-blame. It is especially difficult for the spouse or parents of the suicidee. Grieving follows the same general process as in other deaths, but guilt prolongs recovery.

When a person is planning to kill herself, she often gives clues to friends and family members by dropping subtle hints. Many friends and family members either do not choose to believe, or do not understand, the messages being given. Often, friends have heard the threats or complaints before.

Even if they do hear the message loud and clear, they may not know what to do about it or to whom they can turn for help. They wonder how to prevent the suicide but feel powerless to stop it. Often they deny to themselves and others that such a thing could actually happen, and later the denial is a source of a great deal of guilt and self-blame.

Even though there may have been signals and warning signs prior to the suicide, you could not realize the impact that the actual death would inflict upon you. The suicide of a family member is a triple threat. It is a sudden death, with no time to prepare for your grief; it is the loss of a significant person in your life; and it is an action loaded with emotional content.

You will experience grief over a suicide in the same identifiable stages. In the beginning, you will feel shock, numbness and disbelief. This will last long beyond the funeral.

There is a danger during the first weeks of immersing yourself in denial and repression. But to repress or subdue or restrain any painful thoughts or feelings can delay your natural grieving process. It is crucial that you allow the emotions that come to you to be expressed. If you do not grieve now, you will have to do so later, and you may develop neurotic and/or phobic symptoms as a result, even years after the event.

The funeral is a time to get support from family, friends, and others who may share the pain and anguish of the death. It is an important time to begin to realize the truth of the situation. The funeral is the ritual of separation. It is for you, the living. It is both public and personal acknowledgment of the end of the deceased's life. It's your chance to begin to say goodbye, to begin to let go, to start the rest of your life – as a survivor.

Even if you allow yourself to do the work of grieving as it presents itself to you, it will probably take from one to two years before you feel normal again. It will seem difficult, even impossible, to re-establish an interest in living your life with joy and happiness.

Working through your grief will release you from the bondage of your relationship with the dead person. You have a right to survive. You can survive. And you will have a new strength and sense of value that you never imagined possible. While the pain you will feel will be hell for a while, it can be a gift in disguise: a gift for growth, for a new way of being. George Eliot said, "The strongest principle of growth lies in human choice." *You have a choice.*

After the initial period of shock, bewilderment, and denial, another phase will slowly begin to take over. As the numbness wears off, the reality of the death will creep more and more into your awareness. Your thoughts are likely to be on the dead person. Confusion will prevail. You may feel a certain amount of relief at being out of a "bad" relationship, if there were problems. Now is the time to be glad that the problems are over. Try to do this without guilt or self-blame. Everyone wishes for release from the trials in life from time to time.

You may be uptight about your relationship being held up to public scrutiny. Suicide has a way of exposing private matters to questioning and speculation by others. You may be worried about what others are thinking or saying about you. Try to forget this. It will only prolong your grieving. If people care about you, they will not judge you. People who are not sympathetic to you will not believe any defense you make. It is impossible for everyone to accept and approve of you. Seek your true friends.

Your job now is to survive, not to defend yourself to others. Ask someone you trust to be with you when you feel like talking or crying. If you think others blame you for the death, talk it out, cry it out. Some of what you think others are saying about you may be a projection of what you deeply feel or fear about yourself. If this is so, then it is time for you to get in touch with these thoughts and feelings. Only by bringing them to the surface can you release yourself from them.

This will be a time to break the old habits of the relationship. You can help speed up the process by getting rid of as many reminders as possible, such as clothes, toys, and other pieces of personal property. Rearrange the furniture, or paint and redecorate the room; use it for another purpose. Move into another bedroom, another bed in the house if you slept with that person. Don't destroy all reminders of the person, items such as photographs or special mementos; just put them away for a while. There were good times that you will want to remember later and share with others.

Memorializing the dead loved one is unhealthy and is a form of denial of the reality of the death. To get on with your own life, it is important to get ready to let go of the other person. You must bury him or her psychologically as well as physically. Keeping personal belongings, setting aside a room as a monument, or going to the grave site every day will only prolong your pain and your grief.

During this early time of adjustment there will be difficult issues for you to handle. The police and coroner's office may insist that you attend a public hearing to officially declare the death a suicide. In dealing with insurance agents, you may find that your policy will pay less, or even nothing, in the case of suicide.

If there is a suicide note, you will have to decide what to do with it. The police may have it for a time. Later, keeping it may be a problem – another connection to and reminder of this traumatic episode in your life. Putting it away in a safety deposit box may be a good idea until you are ready to destroy it. Better yet, a ceremonial burning will release you of the problem and serve as a symbol of letting go.

Another difficult issue is how to handle the suicide publicly. Because suicide provokes negative responses from people in general, it is tempting to lie when talking to strangers or people remotely involved in your life. Protect yourself in any way that feels right for you at the time. If it is easier to evade the question than to feel defensive, do so. A lie may catch up with you at some later date, but you don't have to share the details with everyone. One suggestion is simply to say that the event is too close to you and that you would rather not talk about it right now.

My father committed suicide when I was twenty-three years old. For many years I was so ashamed of this that I vowed never to tell my children about the way their grandfather died. I lived in another state and it was easy to hide the fact of his suicide from anyone who might tell them in the future. I never talked about it to friends. I swore my husband to secrecy. For years I lived in the fear that if my children ever found out the truth, it would harm them or the way they felt about me and my family. I wanted them to love their grandfather, even though he died before they were born. As they grew up, I knew they would want to hear stories about their grandfather, and I wanted only good stories to be remembered. Suicide is not a good story.

Finally, after ten or twelve years of my hiding the truth, I told them about his death. To my surprise, they were very nonchalant and unconcerned about the whole thing. It did

not destroy them for life, and they could love him for all of
what they knew about both his life and death. I realized then
that the secret was not really for their sake, but for mine. I
had been ashamed of myself. I felt hurt and angry and guilty.
I felt rejected and abandoned, and I did not know what to do
with these painful feelings, so I buried them inside myself
until I was forced to face them. I was really protecting myself
from accepting the truth of his death.

Guilt is the most difficult emotion to confront. No doubt
you will mentally go over and over the events of the person's
last day, and the days and weeks prior to the death – trying
to make sense of the whole thing, searching for answers,
asking questions that will never be answered or verified
because the only person who can answer them is dead. You
will ask, "Why did he do it?";"Why did she do this to me?";
"Why didn't she tell me things were so bad?"; "Why didn't
he trust me to love and help him?"; "Didn't she think of the
problems this would cause for us?"; "Why didn't he pay
the last premium of the insurance policy?"; "Why couldn't
I stop him?"; "What did I do wrong?"; "Didn't I love her
enough?"; "I should have done something." These and many
other questions will haunt you if you let them. Don't dwell
on them because there are no answers now, only more crazy-
making questions.

Guilt comes from a feeling of regret or remorse, believing
that you have either done something wrong that you wish
you had not done, or that you failed to do something you
think you should have done. You can spend years going
over every argument, every nasty word, every conversation,
punishing yourself for what you should have done or should

have said that might have made a difference. But remorse accomplishes nothing except making you feel worse.

When you feel guilty, you also feel that you are to blame and that you *should* be punished, as if you have committed a crime. We lock criminals away from the rest of society. But no one is going to punish you or lock you away except yourself. And this is not necessary. Guilt is completely unproductive. It will only delay your recovery. Of course it is great for dragging out a desire for self-pity, and any self-destructive feelings or wishes you may have for yourself.

You may feel both relieved and sorry that you are alive and the other person is not. All of these ambivalent feelings are normal and a natural response to this tragedy in your life.

The truth is that, whatever happened in the past, *you did the best that you could at the time.* Now forgive yourself. And then you can begin to get on with your life. If you do not do this, you are continuing to give the memory of your dead loved one all the power over your present life.

Closely connected with guilt are feelings of failure. You may think that you have failed as a friend, as a parent, spouse, or child, but mostly as a human being. You may berate yourself for not being more sensitive to the signals, for not preventing the suicide, for not knowing the seriousness of the threat. Or, in anger, you may have said something like, "You keep threatening to kill yourself; why don't you just go ahead and get it over with?"

You may be searching your soul for your responsibility in the death. Blaming yourself, directly or indirectly, for causing it. Don't worry. These thoughts and feelings are normal and common. In time they will pass. Focus on being gentle and kind to yourself.

Survival Techniques

The period from about three months to one year after the death will be an intense period of emotional turmoil and confusion. One minute you may feel relieved, even euphoric; then you may begin to cry, then feel angry and hostile, depressed and sad. All of these emotions will flood over you. This is a time to be extremely gentle and good to yourself. Allow the emotions to come out and to be expressed. If you do, they will spend themselves and pass sooner.

The next stage you will probably go through will include some feelings of depression and anger. The confusion will begin to clear. Depression comes with the realization that the death really happened. It happened the way it did. And it is final and irreversible. Depression is anger turned inward. You will feel powerless and impotent. There will probably be lingering feelings of guilt and failure that need to be worked through.

Symptoms of depression include sleep problems, listlessness, low energy level, fatigue, decreased interest in sex, poor appetite or eating all the time, feeling low down or sad. There are some anti-depressant drugs on the market that your physician can prescribe for you. They will buy you some time that you may need for the healing process. Recovery is really a matter of time passing and allowing yourself to do the necessary work to get through the process of grieving.

Do not take drugs for your depression if you can possibly

get along without them. Like alcohol and tranquilizers, they are a crutch. You will get through your grief faster if you are fully aware. Occasionally, you may choose something to help you relax and sleep. Antidepressants, unlike many drugs, must be taken for several months to be fully effective, and some have unfavorable side effects. If you do think you would like to take them for a while, read all you can about them, especially the one prescribed for you. You can go to the library and look up any drug in a book called the *PDR (Physician's Desk Reference)*. Doctors use this book all the time. It has information about dosages, manufacturers of the drug, side effects and contraindications. Or check the internet. Google.com is a great resource.

After all, it is *your* body, and you should make an informed decision about taking any drug for a long time. If your doctor has problems with you being informed about your medication, get another doctor. Your doctor is only your employee. He or she should be a consultant to you – not a god.

Other effective, non-prescription ways to handle stress are exercise, massage, spa facilities (steam room, jacuzzi, and swimming pools), and body-work programs such as polarity and reflexology or aerobic exercise classes.

The length of time you will be depressed will depend on the amount of resistance that you have to feeling the necessary sadness, disappointment, and anger that are seething inside of you.

Here is an exercise that may help you address your resistance. Lie down in a quiet place. Relax. Let's try some imagery. Think of resistance as a powerful force against which you stand firm, unyielding, and in opposition. Imagine a door that someone is trying to open from the other side. You have a great fear of whatever is on the other side of that door. So, with all of your might, you push and push to keep that door closed. You may even feel terror and panic if the door opens even a crack. You don't really *know* what is on the other side, but you *think* that it must be bad. You must constantly be vigilant or the door will open. You resist facing your own feelings. How exhausting!

Now, go to the door and try holding it closed with all of your strength. Have someone push to try to open it. Pay attention to your body, to where you hold tension, to the stress and strain of resisting. Pay attention to the focus of your mind, to your thoughts. They are concentrated on the single purpose of keeping the door closed. After a while you don't have the strength to hold it any longer. Your resistance is gone now; you will have to open the door, look at whatever is on the other side, acknowledge your pain and anger and fears.

Imagine that you stop resisting and you open the door a little. What is there? Look at it...listen to it...feel it. It is part of you. Own it. Take it inside. It's okay: you can handle your feelings. Open the door a little at a time. Let in some light (enlightenment), and some fresh air (new ways of being). These changes do not have to be your own private bogeymen, your own private hell!

Sometimes it is necessary to go to the depths of despair to really know that *you are a survivor*. When you do this and come back, you know that you will make it.

It is better to be resilient than resistant. But in order to be resilient, to spring back to your original form, you must stop resisting. The sooner you open the door, the sooner you will release the emotional charge of those painful feelings. Anger is often the most frightening feeling.

Anger at yourself comes from guilt, shame and self-blame. If you are stuck here and feel that you need to be punished, you may be in trouble with self-destructive desires of your own. Get help! These thoughts are common, but they mustn't become more than thoughts. The last thing your family needs now is another suicide!

When the Suicidee is a Spouse

When I asked a client recently about his feelings of anger toward his wife, who had shot herself eleven months ago, he said, "Of course I'm not mad at her. She tried to tell me the night before and I didn't understand. If I had only taken more time to listen to her, she might still be alive today and I wouldn't be here now." He was still struggling with guilt and self-blame. In time, I hope he will move beyond these feelings to get on with his life. He will have to acknowledge that his wife's death created chaos in his life and in the lives of their children. He has many reasons to feel angry at her, but he isn't aware of these feelings yet.

Another client raged, three months after her husband's death, "I am furious at Harry! How could he leave me like this? I have two kids to raise that I really didn't want in the first place; I had them because he wanted kids. He didn't pay the last premium on the insurance policy, and I don't know how I am going to survive financially." At least she can admit her anger and the source of it: her dead husband. Her progress is in the right direction, but she still has to learn what to do with anger, how to let it go, and finally how to forgive Harry and to release him.

Eventually you will think less about the never-to-be-answered questions. You will not continually dwell on her or him; soon, in fact, little of your thinking will be about that event in your life. You will begin to experience pleasure again, alone and with others.

When you can say, "You are dead and I am alive; I release you from my life with love, and now it is time for me to get on with the rest of my life," then you will know you are better.

Releasing your loved one doesn't mean completely erasing the memories of this relationship from your existence. This person and this death are part of your life experience. You may continue to feel twinges of regret and sadness, especially at significant times, like anniversaries. This is normal and to be expected. What is not normal is being so occupied with the memory of the person and the suicide that it continues to interfere with your life after a "reasonable" period of time. A reasonable period of time is between one and two years, with slow progress being made along the way.

Your reaction to the suicide of a loved one, just as your reaction to any other death or major loss, will depend on several factors. These include your personality, the events surrounding the death, the way you have dealt with change and grief in the past, and your relationship with your loved one.

After a suicide, the surviving spouse is often left with a deep sense of failure and confusion, especially when an impulsive or planned suicide is a gesture of anger or hostility, directed at you.

One woman killed herself on her husband's birthday wearing a locket that he had given her as a birthday present. He didn't understand why she did it. He felt that he should have known and been able to prevent her death. Obviously, her act was in anger, a rejection of him. She wanted to hurt him, and she succeeded.

Socially, the widow or widower of a suicidee is more likely to be shunned than to get support from friends and other widows or widowers. He or she is also more likely to feel abandoned and/or rejected. Additional stress may develop from in-laws casting blame for the death.

If you have children, especially young ones, you will have the added burden of helping them through their grief, and resolving conflicts and guilt that they may experience. If possible, find a family member or friend to act as a confidant and support system for each child. Someone they can trust and talk to openly will help you and your children.

Tell their teachers the situation so they can exercise patience and be on the lookout for problems that might surface in school. Don't abdicate your role as a parent, but for a while you will be so preoccupied with your own grief that it will be difficult for you to take good care of the needs of others.

You need all the help you can get. Don't hesitate to ask for the help you need. If you don't let people know you need help, they may be hesitant to offer it, thinking they are interfering. It is up to you to recognize that you need help and to find it. You may not always get it the first time you ask, or from the people you think should respond to your needs. Don't be discouraged. Try again. Be specific about the help that will be best for you and ask for it. Find someone to clean the house, or someone to be a substitute parent for your children for a while, or someone to stay with you at night when you can't bear being alone. Ask for whatever you want or need.

When the Suicidee is a Parent

Young children of a person who commits suicide will have unique issues to deal with. Because their parents are so crucial in their lives, they may be unable to see factors outside themselves as being important to their parents. So they may believe they're responsible for the suicide because they are "bad" or unlovable children. Or they may recall a time when the dead parent was angry with them. They may feel that they "cost" too much if they asked for toys or food while shopping with the parent.

They may have been angry at the parent for some punishment and wished that the parent was either dead or would go away "forever." In this case especially, they may feel that they caused the death. As a result, they may develop a great fear of their own power over life and death. They may have told the parent that they hated him or her, or had such a thought, and as a result end up feeling terribly guilty after the death.

It is extremely important for the child to be able to

remember these incidents and to talk about them in order to release them, to come to understand that he's not responsible for the parent's death. Otherwise, they may lie hidden for a long time and fester, finally erupting years later in behavior that is self-punishing.

Children must be reassured that negative feelings toward parents are often perfectly normal and that such feelings do not cause people to kill themselves.

They must learn that the suicidee – and no one else – made the decision to die for his or her own reasons. Because of the death, children will feel abandoned and rejected. If the child is insecure about being lovable, those feelings will be reinforced by a parent's suicide. It may take a lot of time and patience and professional help to reassure the grieving child that he is valued and worthwhile.

If a child is denying her feelings about the death, she may blame someone else in the family – often the living parent – for the death. Of course, this is a difficult problem for the entire family. It may be necessary to get outside professional help to clean up the relationships.

Like the surviving spouse, children often feel that they could or should have been able to prevent the suicide. They may think that rescue attempts should have been more effective to reverse the death and to save the parent. The image of the dead parent may haunt them for years in dreams and daydreams, especially if the death was a violent one or if they saw the body.

The age of the child at the time of the death will make a difference in memories, guilt, fears and overall effects.

Every child will have issues to deal with before he is free of the trauma and stigma of a parental suicide.

If a child strongly identified with the parent, it is likely that he will have suicide fantasies of his own, especially as he approaches the age the parent was when he died. Such children – even as adults – may fear and, at the same time, entertain thoughts of ending their own life in a similar way.

Phobias may develop that are closely related to the death of the parent, such as a fear of guns, drugs, or heights. Sometimes physical symptoms develop that are similar to the way a parent died, like getting choking feelings if the parent hanged herself, or having trouble breathing if the parent inhaled lethal fumes.

Rosalie, a client of mine, started to prepare a will and to plan for the distribution of her property at the age of thirty-one. Her activity was compulsive rather than planned. She didn't know why she was doing it, but she felt that she had to. For about six months before her thirty-second birthday, she grew increasingly restless, and thought off and on about how her family would get along without her. She occasionally had thoughts about being dead. She didn't consciously think about killing herself.

As her birthday approached, she had an anxiety attack during which she was assailed by confused, undefined fears. In exploring her past, she revealed that her mother committed suicide at the age of thirty-two. Subconsciously, she thought she would end her life in the same way. When she was able to bring the hidden fears to the surface and handle them, she was extremely relieved to reach her thirty-second birthday.

When the Suicidee is a Child

The parents of a child who kills himself live with a profound sense of failure as well as feelings of guilt. They blame themselves and each other for the death. I recently heard of a thirteen-year-old boy who hanged himself. Next to his body was the report card that he got at school that day. He had received a D grade in one subject and couldn't face the disapproval of his father, who encouraged and expected excellence in his son. A brief note said, "Dad, I'm sorry I let you down."

If the child is an adult, the parents may project blame onto other factors, such as the demands of college, the job, or a wife or husband.

Surviving children are sometimes encouraged to take the place of the dead one: "Well, John got into a good college; you can too." The surviving child may be identified with the deceased one: "You hold your fork just like John did." Sometimes the dead child is seen as a hero: "It takes a lot of guts to knock yourself off." Occasionally, families will try to make reparation by giving money to a worthy cause, such as a suicide prevention program or a student counseling service in a college.

One of the biggest tragedies is that such a death often drives a wedge into family relationships instead of bringing people together. Everyone in a family suffers over any death, but death by self-destruction is even more difficult to understand and come to terms with.

I encourage you to turn to the people who are closest to you for support. Talk together; cry and mourn together.

Compare feelings, reactions, anger and frustration. So often family members withdraw into themselves or go their separate ways when tragedy strikes, instead of sharing the grief and supporting each other. It is easier to work out your feelings of guilt, failure, and blame with loving support.

Forgive and begin to live again. Don't run away from your pain or from your loved ones. This is the time that you really need each other. Risk reaching out and asking for the love and care that you need now, and be available to give the same loving and caring to others. Get beneath the surface of re-living the details and talk about your feelings, fears, and frustrations.

For a while, survival will be just an effort to get through one day at a time. Some days will be better than others. Slowly, gradually, time will pass and you will heal. Be good to yourself. Be kind to yourself. You have more to do in life, and you must survive to do it.

The Mystery of Suicide

Most suicides result from a combination of factors. When someone has had enough of life, it's difficult to identify any one reason for death. Sometimes a change can be a crisis event that precipitates suicidal behavior. Such potentially dangerous events might be the threat or actual loss of a loved one through death; separation or divorce; changes in self-image, as may occur in an accident of rape or beating; loss of a job; sudden illnesses and hospitalization; loss of motivation or energy to start over or to renew the missing part of one's life.

Most people have thought of suicide at least once in their

lifetime. But why do we all think about it and only a few of us do it? For those who attempt and/or complete suicide, the big difference is that they have closed the gap in the thinking process. That is, they actually see themselves as dead now, not in the future. They see their lives as already over, and the actual death is an "after the fact" action.

Suicide presents more questions than answers, especially for the survivor trying to understand the puzzle of a suicide. It is complicated and frightening. Probably no one who has not seriously attempted suicide can fully understand why someone would go through with it, but there are some common patterns.

It's when whatever is most important in one's life seems to be missing, destroyed or unattainable that life seems no longer worth the effort. Why go on living when there is more pain than pleasure? There are feelings of helplessness and powerlessness. Perhaps anger turned inward.

Depression plays an important part in suicide. Many suicides are committed while a person is just beginning to come out of a depression.

When no single event seems to be the trigger, there has probably been a long period of depression or dissatisfaction about something crucial.

Before making the decision to kill oneself, most people go through a crisis in problem solving. During this process, there is an increase of tension and confusion as solutions continue to be elusive. More feelings of disorganization and the inability to sort out positive solutions and choices for the future lead to greater levels of frustration. The lack of success in resolving the tension with familiar problem-solving techniques leads to helplessness and hopelessness.

When the problem continues, the person may see death as the only way out of the dilemma. The state of prolonged tension may last a few hours to a few months, or even longer. It may be combined with other emotional reactions such as anxiety, chaos, panic, sadness, a sense of loss, depression, denial and repression of thoughts and feelings, excessive fantasies, hope for a better life on a spiritual plane, or a sense of deprivation.

If the feelings of isolation and worthlessness continue, with no visible hope or sign of things getting better, suicide may be the result. In the worst moments of despair, the person feels totally alone and has no sense of identity or worth. "No one understands me. No one loves me. No one ever will, because I am unlovable."

Suicide has been called the ultimate cry for help. It is also the ultimate act of anger. It is the final rejection and punishment of oneself, society and all others concerned. The threat of suicide can be used as a tool for manipulation. Death by suicide can have incredible power over the lives of the survivors. Family, relatives, friends, neighbors, co-workers, boss, and others are left with pain, confusion, and sometimes guilt over the death. They have no choice except to live with their grief and all of their unanswered questions.

Ambivalence characterizes the thoughts of those contemplating suicide. They want both to live and to die, to be out of their present misery and pain, and sometimes to punish those who they think caused it. These mixed motivations are seen in the suicide notes that express both love and hate, anger and regret, fear and hopelessness.

These opposing impulses to live and die are often expressed in suicide attempts. Someone swallows a bottle of pills, then calls for help before slipping into unconsciousness. However, if a person acts self-destructively during agitation or under the influence of alcohol or drugs, there may be a sense of unreality to the event, and a call for help may not come, or may come too late.

When an act is impulsive, especially in anger, one doesn't fully think through the reality of the consequence. Rather, the desire for revenge or a wish to induce guilt in another person is the primary motive, and it is accompanied by a reckless disregard for the finality of death.

Some people take their own lives rather than go through a terminal disease. They are trying to avoid pain, or do not wish to burden their families with the expense and grief of watching them die a slow death. Many elderly suicidees feel that death is preferable to the physical deterioration, isolation, and loneliness that are so often dreaded by those who have outlived family and friends. Living out their final days in a nursing home is not a pleasant choice. Making a rational decision about when and how to die is a preferable option.

For some people, suicide is a well thought out, rational decision. Perhaps in these cases, it is truly a choice to exercise the right to make a decision about one's own life. For other people, it is a reaction to incredible stress, fear and depression – an act of desperation. In these cases, it is not a rational "action," but a "reaction" to intolerable circumstances currently operating in the life of a person.

Almost every town in the United States has a crisis intervention center where a person who is feeling desperate can call and talk to caring people. These crisis workers are trained to talk to those who are thinking about suicide. If you or someone close to you is talking about suicide, or giving verbal or non-verbal clues about self-destructive impulses, contact your local HELP LINE or Suicide Prevention Service (names vary from city to city). They can refer you to competent counseling, talk you through the immediate crisis, or console a family member. For the suicidal individual, it is important to restore hope and a sense of worth, and to recall former times of strength and hope.

Social Stigma of Suicide

Family members are stunned and wounded by a suicide, and their plight is often worsened by curiosity and the judgments of other relatives, neighbors and fellow workers. They have no answers to "Why?" Support may not be as forthcoming as it is for another type of death. The only real place to seek solace may be in a group of Survivors of Suicide. The more homogeneous the group, the more its members can understand and relate to the circumstances of your situation.

A Modest Proposal

Perhaps the tragedy of impulsive suicide could be prevented if we had a method of allowing people to die, so long as the person who wished to die agreed to a few conditions. We could create a place like the "Diatorium" portrayed in the movie *Soylent Green*, where family and friends could be there to say good-bye. The conditions imposed would be that the would-be suicidee would have to agree to undergo 48 hours of extensive counseling or therapy before the suicide could be authorized and completed.

Many impulsive suicides would be prevented if the distraught person had someone to point out other options, to underscore the finality of the decision, and to remind the person of the pain family members would experience after the death.

Personal Control of Your Death

For those who want some say in decisions about their death, the Living Will (now called an Advanced Directive) allows you some minimal choices in your own death. You can choose not to have "heroic" medical methods to keep you alive – respirators, feeding tubes and other mechanical means of prolonging life, especially if you are brain dead – or any other aid that would prevent your dying with dignity without extensive medical intervention to extend life beyond the time a natural death would occur.

These forms can be obtained from most attorneys who specialize in estate planning, or at your local hospital. I filled one out and signed it when I had knee replacement surgery, and it is on file at the hospital. These documents change often and it is important that you keep yours updated and current if you want to maintain control over your choices in your death. As I write this section in 2007, there are changes taking place almost hourly and in ways that vary from state to state.

The Netherlands, Belgium and the State of Oregon are

the only jurisdictions in the world where the law permits euthanasia or physician-assisted suicide. Many other states in the United States have "right-to-die" movements, but at this time they are in various stages of flux, organization and disorganization. Yet those dedicated to the right-to-die concept keep working to educate the public and legislators, and are determined to get laws passed in their favor. They need volunteers and funding to move forward with their cause.

Proponents of physician-assisted suicide won a major victory when the Supreme Court of the United States upheld the legality of the Oregon law in January 2006 in the case of Gonzales vs. Oregon.

A Sample of a Living Will

To My Family Physician, My Lawyer, and All Others Whom It May Concern:

Death is as much a reality as birth, growth, maturity and old age – it is the one certainty of life. If the time comes when I can no longer take part in decisions for my own future, let this statement stand as an expression of my wishes and directions, while I am still of sound mind.

If the situation should arise in which there is no reasonable expectation of my recovery from extreme physical or mental disability, I direct that I be allowed to die and not be kept alive by medications, artificial means or "heroic measures." I do, however, ask that medication be mercifully administered to me to alleviate suffering even though this may shorten my remaining life.

This statement is made after careful consideration and is in accordance with my strong convictions and beliefs. I want the wishes and directions here expressed carried out to the extent permitted by law. Insofar as these provisions are not legally enforceable, I hope that those to whom this Will is addressed will regard themselves as morally bound by my wishes.

(Optional specific provisions to be made in this space.)

DURABLE POWER OF ATTORNEY (optional)

I hereby designate_____ to serve as my attorney-in-fact for the purpose of making medical treatment decisions. This power of attorney shall remain effective in the event that I become incompetent or otherwise unable to make such decisions for myself.

(Either have your signature notarized or have two witnesses sign and date the document.)

Optional Notarization

Witness

Witness

Notary Public (seal)

CHAPTER ELEVEN

YOUR COPING STYLE

It is impossible to live without experiencing grief. Life and grief go hand-in-hand. They are entwined in the intricate web of human existence. We are involved constantly in the flow of change, and change is often connected with loss. Loss requires readjustment to a new set of beliefs, values, circumstances or concept of self. The process of grieving is the way that we release the old ways of thinking and being, and make room for the new ones. It is the way we heal after a loss.

Daily we are confronted with new ideas, products, and different ways of doing things. While integrating these changes, we experience loss as we let go of the familiar. We grieve in a small way for what we know, or for what we had, or for a person who was important in our life. Ending and beginning, birth and death, starts and finishes – these are the unavoidable rhythms and cycles that make life a totally dynamic, ever-changing process.

Life's Crises

Sometimes the events that create change in our lives are low-key and subtle. Our children grow; we learn new skills on our job; our bodies age. We don't even realize that we have changed. Other events are thunderous. They come roaring at us with such a rumble and boom that we don't know what hit us for a while. Life crises like separations, divorces, illness and death are such events, especially if they are unexpected.

Many of the events in life that create major emotional problems are normal transitions from one period to another. But they affect us strongly because of the changes they produce. We call them *crises* because they require a long period of introspection and re-evaluation of self identity, values, and beliefs. Adolescence, getting married, starting a new job, changing careers, mid-life issues including menopause and climacteric (for men), and retirement are all periods of major trauma and change. These transitions are often characterized by long periods of discontent, distress and discomfort.

During these times, we search for answers to internal questions about the meaning of life, relationships, work, social pressures, and so on. Crisis is often a turning point in life, when we formulate new answers and priorities. And as our lives take new direction, it is inevitable that something or someone from the past will be left behind. Changes that are part of a normal life cycle always include loss. Even positive changes such as getting married or starting a new job include loss of past status of being single or unemployed.

In addition, life holds other crises in the form of death,

divorce, separation, accidents, rape, abandonment, fires, and other events that we view as tragic disruptions in the flow of life. In some cases, we are forewarned of the event. With a long terminal illness, we have time to anticipate what our lives will be like without the sick person. We can begin to grieve before the death occurs. A loved one's death is a major life change, and prior knowledge can give you precious time to more slowly and thoroughly adjust to the inescapable loss.

However, when the crisis is unexpected, as in the case of a sudden death or accident, or an unanticipated conflict, the trauma may be so great that you will undergo an extended period of instability and confusion. Your former life will be gone forever; you can never go back. Your experience will change you, for better or worse, and you will never be exactly the same as you were. How well you acknowledge and manage the changes and losses will decide how comfortably you will proceed into the future.

Most Americans believe that life is generally stable. When we talk about change, we're thinking of the small changes that affect everyday life indirectly. A new product advertised on television, a Supreme Court decision, a foreign war, or who is winning in the playoffs are typical topics of conversation. We're comfortable discussing changes in politics, sports, or entertainment. But when tragedy strikes a friend or acquaintance, the news is passed on in hushed tones, perhaps couched in sympathy, and with relief that it isn't you. Often we don't know what to say to the people who are affected. It's hard to deal with personal changes in ourselves or our friends.

Big changes and small changes occur all the time. Life is full of surprises; some are considered good, others bad. Because we've had painful experiences with change, or know of the crisis events of others, most people see change as threatening.

When a crisis event happens in life, many people try to deny it and to resist. They see the change as an enemy to their stability. The uncertainty of *life after change* often creates resistance and anxiety. Yet crises and other major life events that force you to change can also lead to growth-producing, positive development.

It is natural for the human organism to try to avoid pain and to look for balance. We act as if we have the option of never experiencing change and loss and grief. But we do not have that choice. The issue is how well we respond to changes. Even though we think that we prefer total stability, life would be pretty boring without differences and changes. Every one of us will live through normal life transitions, and we will also experience our share of other crises.

Adjustment to Change

There are at least four possible responses to change. Let's look at them in detail.

Conservation

The first is conservation. This is an attempt to conserve, to protect the status quo, to deny and shut out the anguish of the present pain by trying – at least mentally – to remain in the present or to return to the past. The past is idealized as the remembered state of perfect balance and harmony, a safe refuge.

This is the rigid position of the stoic who only endures the present by denying what precipitated the current crisis. The person who uses conservation as a coping stance is likely to look for others to blame as a way to understand the event. This person is unlikely to take the opportunity to alter existing behavior patterns, beliefs, or values. Passive people often use conservation as their coping style.

Polly took care of her elderly mother until her mother died at age eighty-nine. They lived in the same house where Polly grew up, and after her mother's death Polly continued to live there. She kept her mother's furniture, dishes and pictures and continued most of the activities and associations that her mother enjoyed.

Polly responded to her mother's death with conservation. She never stopped to think whether she wanted to continue her life in the same way. Rather than face her own needs or desires, or evaluate her feelings about her mother, she continued in the same life, as though nothing had changed.

Revolution

The *revolution* response is to suddenly reject former values and beliefs. Security from the past seems contrived and inauthentic. The revolt may be against familiar people, ideas, places, society or objects. It is another way of denying the present pain and anguish, but a more active reaction than conservation. Conservation pulls inward rigidly, tightly seeking safety and security. Like a clam, the passive person shuts himself inside an emotional shell. Revolution, on the other hand, thrusts outwardly, often angrily and aggressively, rejecting the past, denying the present and damning the future.

The person who reacts to the crisis in a revolutionary way is likely to throw himself into a job, or work for a cause with limitless energy and zeal, often repressing thoughts and feelings that are connected to the internal process of grieving.

Such a person rebels and fights against everything that formerly provided stability in life, and becomes dangerously detached from all of the familiar anchors. This can eventually result in extreme anxiety and internal stress shown in a search for new anchors, new values and new meaning in life, with no ongoing sense of self. He is adrift, alone and afraid.

Kent's wife died after a brief illness, leaving him alone at age fifty-one for the first time in his life. Her death made him aware of his mortality and aging, and he was determined not to spend his remaining years alone. He began going out quite often, to parties and nightclubs. He learned to dance and dated women much younger than himself. He stayed so busy with his new social life that he didn't develop any true, deep relationships or consider how he really wanted to spend his time. His behavior was a revolution from his former lifestyle, but he has not yet faced the important question of who he is.

Escape

The third possible response to change is escape. It is a way of evading the present anguish and pain by turning to dependency-inducing chemical or behavioral alternatives. Increased use of alcohol, drugs, sleep, food, or other addictive patterns are some ways of escaping. People who want to escape may join a cult, obsess about one physical illness after another, get caught up in a social whirl, or find some other mindless way to avoid facing and accepting the uncertainty of the present and the pain of the past. This coping style is often used by a person who is passive-aggressive in daily interactions. He or she is fearful, insecure, manipulative, resentful, revengeful, indirect and often gives double messages. A person using this coping style tries to gain what is wanted without taking responsibility for her behavior.

This person wants to turn self-responsibility over to anyone who will assume the position of telling her when, where, and how to live life. The escaper lives as a dependent, scared child, looking for parents to take control of her life for her. They are the martyrs and the victims in society. They want to be rescued; yet when someone suggests a solution, they resent it. This approach to life is perhaps the most difficult to change. In order to alter the pattern of escape, it is necessary to stop reacting to events in life by using escape mechanisms, and to begin to act in new positive ways that are in your own best interest. Developing self-control and self-discipline is an important key for a person who wants to stop escaping and deal with reality.

Jacqueline's husband died unexpectedly, leaving the family financial picture unresolved. Jacqueline didn't know anything about the family's finances or her husband's business, and she trusted his attorney and accountant to sort out his estate. When she received only a small amount of money, she believed the two associates had deliberately cheated her. But, still feeling helpless to take matters into her own hands, she let the matter drop. Now, years later, she complains about "what they did to me," but when she is asked why she didn't fight, she just shrugs: "What could I do?" Jacqueline has escaped responsibility for her problems and allowed others to set the rules in her life.

In order to break the patterns of dependence, begin by developing a reflective consciousness. Do not simply react to the crisis events in life in an instinctive, nonthinking, irrational way. Use such opportunities to reflect, think, and analyze your feelings. Decide on a positive way to resolve the problem.

Learn to Be a Survivor

Crisis events in life test our survival instincts and call upon learned coping styles of conservation, revolution or escape. Emotional reactions in human beings are connected to our most basic need to survive and to the primitive fight-or-flight instincts of our animal nature. But what separates us from other animals is our ability to think, to analyze, to apply knowledge and intelligence to our decisions. Thinking gives us choices. Lower animals are at the mercy of their instincts. Human beings sometimes act the same way, as if they were solely at the mercy of their knee-jerk reactions to events in their lives.

In cases of severe emotional shock, the first response is instinctive, at the emotional level. We want to deny or run away. In time, however, during the process of grieving, the emotional grip eases and our rational minds take over so that we can come to terms with our pain and begin to take control of our lives once again.

At this point we begin to think and act rationally, intelligently, as opposed to reacting blindly, irrationally and emotionally to the circumstances of our lives. We begin to break free of our destructive coping patterns.

Another Response

The fourth way to respond to crisis in life is considerably different from the first three. It is a more flexible, roll-with-the-punches way to deal with life's challenges. This position requires an openness to change and loss, which are viewed as opportunities to gain more depth as a person, to discover more about one's self. It requires a commitment to believing that life is a process: that uncertainty is expected, that change and flux are the norm. It requires a confidence in the undiscovered parts of oneself, and a belief that one has the necessary resources to endure any life crisis.

This openness to change requires the knowledge or belief that no matter how painful the circumstances, you can feel despair and anguish and survive. The person committed to change and survival knows that she will not perish in fear and hopelessness. She sees herself as a cork floating in a stream, sometimes basking in sunny tranquility and calm, other times caught up in its rapids, and now and then, suddenly plunged over a waterfall. But in the end, she is still the same cork, perhaps a little battered and bruised for the travels in life. Her basic essence is unchanged, enduring. And still floating, not drowned.

Transcendence

This is the position of *transcendence*. It means that you can go beyond grief and loss to reorganize your life in a new and meaningful way. The transcendent position requires a commitment to a here-and-now view of the world. It is living in the present with honesty, openness and flexibility to change. We cannot change the past and we don't know the future. All we really have is right now.

Being transcendent means trusting yourself to survive any situation, from small embarrassments to major crises. It means allowing yourself to make mistakes; to fail; to not be perfect; to explore your feelings; to search for your needs and desires; to ask for what you want from others; to stand up for yourself when necessary; to love unconditionally; to give and take; and to learn from your mistakes. Begin to recognize your human rights, take responsibility for yourself and act assertively in your own best interests.

The transcendent position requires a total, complete involvement in life, as opposed to the fear, denial, rebellion and withdrawal of the other three methods of coping.

Compared to the other three patterns of coping and response, transcendence strengthens and comforts you. It is a more fully human way of being than denying, resisting, escaping and refusing to think and feel. You are secure in the knowledge that no matter what happens, the essence of yourself will survive because you are important.

Learning to Transcend

We all use elements of these four positions to varying degrees whenever we cope with difficulties in our lives, but one of the responses will be your predominant one. If your style of coping with change in the past has not always been best for you, you can grow to experience new dimensions of yourself that you may never have dreamed were part of you. You will discover untapped reservoirs of strength and other resources.

How do you learn transcendence? By following the suggestions throughout this book. And by always reminding yourself that no matter what or who is gone, you must heal and survive and go on to the future.

To begin learning transcendence, Polly might take a trip or sell the family home and look for a new place to live. Kent could look for a good friend with whom to discuss his feelings about aging and start to set some goals for the next few years. Jacqueline could take legal action against the people she thinks cheated her.

Or she could forget that chapter in her life and set about finding a way to support herself and focus on events in the present rather than the past.

All three could at least consider these options and take action on one of them when they feel ready.

Avoid Stressful Overload

Every change poses a threat to stability. Death and separation are major disruptive changes. It is more difficult when several changes come at once. Moving to a new town is an example of a complete disruption. Finding a new home, getting a job, enrolling the children in a new school, looking for doctors, dentists, accountants, and so on can be exhausting and frustrating. When such a move closely follows a death or divorce, too much of your former stability is disrupted and it is necessary to regain balance as soon as possible.

Try to monitor and regulate the number and degree of disruptions in your life at any one time. If you are headed for a stress overload, try to delay major changes for a while.

Otherwise, you may be setting yourself up for sickness. It takes patience, practice and time to change.

Be kind to yourself. As you learn to be more aware of your value, more self-confident, more willing to listen and share, others will respond to you with respect, cooperation and appreciation for your openness and honesty.

CHAPTER TWELVE

HANDLING LOSS

Death and separation are two of the major losses that an individual may experience. The chart on page 135 explains the Relative Positions of Loss to ourselves, our fundamental identity. The closer the relationship to the Self, the more disruptive the loss.

The most profound loss is the death of oneself, or a radical change in your body, such as losing your eyesight or a limb, or a deteriorating physical illness like cancer, multiple sclerosis or others that affect physical appearance or stamina. The second most severe type of loss is separation from significant people in our lives by death, divorce, and abandonment. Physical attacks such as mugging or rape can be emotionally devastating, depending on the individual and on the circumstances of the event. A physical accident that requires a long recovery is also a severe loss to the Self.

The third kind of loss requiring adjustment to new ways includes the normal developmental changes of life. Some examples are adolescence, starting and/or ending school, moving to a different place, marriage, retirement, aging-related changes like losing hair, reduced energy, or becoming a grandparent.

The fourth area is loss of important objects, money, hopes, aspirations, or expectations, as well as changes in the social environment such as a Supreme Court decision that may affect your life, giving up a pet project, getting fired, or changing residences.

With every loss we grieve. The grief is usually in appropriate proportion to the severity of the loss. When the grief is out of proportion, you may find that the release of emotions is for a former grief or for an accumulation of losses that have not been handled and resolved.

Grieving is the normal response to the pain and anguish of loss. It is the process of healing after a disruptive loss occurs in life.

It is uncomfortable, painful, a state of dis-ease; if it is not experienced, if it is repressed or denied and internalized, it can lead to serious emotional and/or physical disease. Knowing what to expect in the process of grieving for yourself and others helps you get through the process.

We each have a unique way to grieve. There are subtle differences in our reactions, in the timing, and in the ways we approach and move through the stages of grieving.

It is impossible to be a passive observer of your own pain. It will hurt, and you will have to feel the pain to get past it. To learn your unique way of experiencing loss, pay attention to the way you handle smaller losses in your life. The next time you feel disappointed or irritated, watch your emotional and physical responses.

Pay attention to your thoughts and to the timing. This information will be invaluable to you when you have to adjust to a major crisis. Observe how you respond to change. Do you try to deny the loss or blame someone? Do you place obstacles in the path to healing? You may want to alter your process the next time you have to handle a loss. *Get to know yourself.*

The extent of the trauma that a loss will produce is usually related to four important factors. *First,* to the degree of the emotional bond that you have with the lost person, place, or thing; *second,* to the type of loss; *third,* to your personality and to the way you have handled previous losses; and *fourth,* to the timing and prior knowledge of the loss. Let's look briefly at each of these factors in greater detail.

Degree of Emotional Bond

Obviously the greatest loss that we can experience is our own death. The most intense and often most confused emotional relationship of our life is with our self. The emotional relationship that we have with another person, place, or object is connected to the amount of dependency between us. Dependency is based on our basic survival needs, including the physical, emotional, mental, and spiritual aspects of our lives.

Every significant loss is like the loss of a part of ourselves in death. A great part of the fear in all losses stems, at least subconsciously, from the threat to our own survival. If we depend on a special person to take care of some of our needs, then the actual or threatened loss of that person causes a great disruption in our life, a fear that we can't go on.

If our self-image or identity is based on another person's opinion of us, loss of him may be overwhelming. This is especially true if you have been only a reflection of what he saw or wanted to see in you, and you haven't had a firm sense of who you really are on your own. If you have been emotionally, financially, socially, and/or physically dependent on another, the loss of that person will be very hard to handle for a while. Before you can recover, you must learn to meet your own needs.

Consider the death of a parent. A five-year-old child is dependent in every way on his mother. If she dies, he may not understand why his mother is no longer there to bathe him, help him dress, prepare his meals, read to him at night, and kiss his tears away. Such a loss is total for the child. It threatens his sense of survival in a real way: others will have to take his mother's place in order for him to go on living.

Now think of the death of a parent for a forty-five year-old woman. When her mother dies, there may be great feelings of sadness and a sense of loss, but she is likely to have left her mother's home years earlier and probably has a family of her own. She has her own circle of friends and her own means of financial support. Her mother no longer meets her primary needs. Therefore, the impact of her mother's death will be very different for her than for a five-year-old child.

The case is similar in the death of a spouse. If a woman

has been out in the world working, earning money, and has her own friends, she is likely to adjust more easily when her life is disrupted by the death of her husband. She has been less dependent on her husband to meet *all* of her needs. On the other hand, a woman who has always stayed at home, and whose friends have been related to her husband's work or interests, may find that during early widowhood she will have a greater adjustment to make. She will not have a stable support system to lean on, and she will have to learn to develop unfamiliar survival skills such as finding and holding a job, managing financial matters, etc. She is less likely to have a strong sense of herself to build on. She will need to develop many new skills rather quickly and under more stressful circumstances.

The same may be said for a man whose wife took care of all his physical needs, like shopping, cooking, cleaning, washing clothes, and keeping on top of the bills. He now needs to learn to do these things for himself and become self-sufficient.

Type of Loss

The type of loss also determines your response. Losing a special person in your life has one effect, while losing an important place such as a neighborhood, city, school, or place of employment affects us differently. Other types of losses may have to do with material objects such as a car, a home, furniture, recreational equipment, photographs, jewelry, or objects that have sentimental value. Changes in physical appearance can be considered a special type of loss. Aging-related changes, accidents, or surgical procedures that leave scars are losses that affect a person's self-image.

Another type of loss is the loss of a role. Roles are the most common ways that we define ourselves in our culture. Marital status, the type of job you have, and the level of your education are all examples of social roles.

You may feel lost or confused because the role of wife or husband is no longer available to supply you with a sense of identification. The effect of role loss may be influenced by whether or not the loss is replaceable. If your wife dies, her role as wife can be filled by another woman; but the woman who was your wife is not replaceable. Some comfort and love come with the new relationship, but there may always be feelings of missing the dead person. The stronger the emotional connection, the harder the loss is to replace.

The same is true if you move to a new house. The house and neighborhood have been replaced, but not with the same room location, memories, and familiar problems as the old house had. Your new house may have all the conveniences you need, but you miss the old house because of what it means to you.

If your house is burglarized and your television is stolen, it is easily replaced. Yet some objects with sentimental value are irreplaceable. Sentimental attachments are emotional attachments reminding us of special people, places or events from our past. This kind of loss is often much more upsetting than a large financial loss. It's the loss of something close to your emotional self.

Personality and Previous Losses

The third factor in how you handle loss is concerned with your personality and the way that you have managed previous losses in your life. We discussed some of these different ways of adjusting to change earlier. Let us emphasize here that almost everybody has some resistance to the pain associated with losses in their lives. We all wish that the discomfort and hurt would just go away and that life would get *back to normal*. But this won't happen. We cannot go backward. New norms will slowly emerge. Resistance only delays and drags out the inevitable.

When the loss is severe enough, resisting your healing process can lead to serious consequences. Physically, more energy is needed to fight and to deny emotional feelings than to release them. Let yourself cry, or yell, or scream to get rid of the stored-up feelings. Your feelings will try to surface over and over in the form of sadness or anger. Experience them. Feel them. Remember, current losses are magnified by the pain of former losses.

For example, depression is one of the serious problems associated with aging. Depression results from anger turned inward and from feelings of helplessness. Yet not all older people get depressed. Those who are chronically depressed have an accumulation of unresolved losses.

During life we experience many losses. If each one is handled as it presents itself, we can grow in the knowledge that a new loss won't devastate us. We can and will survive – hopefully, in a stronger and more integrated way. The person who ages successfully is one who bounces back after a loss and is able to continue living an effective and happy life.

The same is true for everyone; age, in fact, has little to do with effectively handling the losses in our lives. An infant who is suddenly weaned from the breast or his cherished thumb experiences a profound loss. The infant grieves, perhaps in a way that will become a lifelong pattern.

Birth, in fact, is the first great loss in our lives. It is a loss of a safe environment – where the temperature is perfectly controlled, food is supplied, and other needs are met effortlessly. Then suddenly we are abruptly discharged and ejected from the womb. Birth is extremely traumatic. No wonder some babies are born crying.

Experts think that the way we cope and adjust to painful events is established at the time of birth and on an unconscious level. And one of the challenges of our lives is to learn new and more effective ways to handle painful incidents – to live through them more consciously.

Remember, we are all unique. Observe the way you handle changes, disappointments, and small losses in your life. If your process is negative and unpleasant, begin to change yourself. We all have the capacity to change. Learn to transcend. The first step is to be aware, reflect, and decide how you want to be. Think positively. Be a survivor. Set goals. Then do it. If you feel overwhelmed, get professional help.

Anticipatory Grief: Timing and Prior Knowledge

Knowing about a death or loss before it happens is an advantage. It gives you a chance to prepare for the change, and to do some of the work of grieving before the actual event occurs. While your loved one is dying, you may anticipate what your life will be like without her or him. It is like rehearsing for the changes that you are soon to experience. You can anticipate the absence while still giving important time and attention to your loved one's last days.

This is a small grieving process. If you are extremely dependent on this person for your physical or emotional survival, your feelings of threat and fear may be profound. You may experience loneliness and separation anxiety even before the death.

Although it is extremely painful to watch someone you love suffer, knowledge that a loved one has a terminal disease allows you both the opportunity to complete the business in the relationship and to say goodbye. Emotional preparation before the death can reduce the long-term impact of grief work after the death. However, not everyone takes advantage of anticipatory grief; they will have to do all of their grief work after the death occurs.

In the case of a sudden death, there is no opportunity to prepare yourself for the loss of the person and the relationship. Therefore, all of the grief work must take place after the death, and recovery usually takes longer.

Separation

Separation is the critical event, whether it is caused by death, divorce or abandonment. The moment of leave-taking is the most traumatic time. The more time you have before the separation, the better. In all relationships where bonds of love are present, there is an element of loss when it ends.

Even with prior knowledge, the moment of the final separation is traumatic. It is the end of one chapter in your life and the beginning of another. Separation brings a major change, beginning with the process of healing from the loss.

Mini separations can prepare you for major ones. You may recognize anxiety, fear or feeling threatened when a loved person is absent. This can happen when your spouse is away on a business trip, or when your children are out at night, or when older children leave for college or move to another city, or when someone you love does not get home at an appointed time. Often a little twinge will surface and you will begin to worry. This is commonly called separation anxiety.

Choosing Life

Kings and slaves alike – and all the rest of us, too – experience life as a dynamic process. It is filled with times of peace, joy, tranquility, disappointment, anger, hurt, fear, love, and much more. It is ever-changing, always in flux. Pleasure and pain are the extremes. And at some time in our lives, we experience both.

Many people live their lives somewhere safely between the extremes, resisting change and risking little.

We each experience life with a different cast of characters, and a plot and script that vary a little from other people's. If we could step outside of the drama of our own life and view it as if we were sitting in the audience watching a play unfold before us, we probably would either be bored, feel impatient at the absurdity of the interactions of the actors, laugh or cry.

Sometimes we are moved to tears of sympathy for a sad event. In drama, human crisis is often the beginning of the play. We watch to see how the solution to tragedy will be resolved. We hope it will have a happy ending.

Often, if we are detached from personal involvement in the process of our own lives, we experience life – the drama of events – only intellectually. Without feelings, we remain detached and uninvolved. We watch our own lives as if we were watching a play. We become spectators instead of actors in – or, better yet, authors of – our own lives.

If you are detached from life, are you really alive? To be alive means to be in a state of action. Imagine yourself back in the picture. Remember *you* are the star, not the detached objective viewer. Your intellect does not work alone, but in conjunction with the *whole* of yourself – your physical sensations and your emotions.

In the drama of everyone's life, tragedy strikes. It is absolutely unavoidable. Trouble or stress may take many shapes and forms. It may be a separation from a loved one through death or divorce, or just a short vacation. It may be seeing a child die. It may be losing an object that has a special meaning in your life. It may be coming to terms with your own aging process, or moving to another town, or making a hard decision about your career. It may be the death by suicide of your spouse, or having a disease or an accident that suddenly leaves you partially paralyzed.

We all have such events to cope with in our lives. Vary the script a little, change the names and places and details. We all get something to resolve. In fact, we get several somethings. In life's course, each of us has many tragedies, crises, and events that are difficult and painful.

The most significant difference among us is in the way we react and respond to these events. The process of readjustment is called the *grieving process.* A process is a progressive course, a series of measures or changes that get you from one place (psychologically) to another. It is the opportunity to be *progressive.* Tragically, some people choose to meet the painful events in their lives *regressively:* by denying, not changing, not facing the loss.

Because grieving is a process, you will naturally move forward and progress if you just relax and go with it. On the other hand, if you resist and fight the work of grief, you will eventually break down physically, mentally or, in time, both ways.

Grief is like the Odyssey of Ulysses, full of the unknown, through uncharted territory and internal battles, and accompanied by fears of losing control and of going crazy.

All human beings have to experience difficult events in life. No one escapes living without pain in the area of love and relationships. We all lose a loved one through death eventually. Grandparents and parents generally die before we do. Some people lose a spouse, a child, or a sibling. Loss hurts, more than anything else you'll experience.

This severing by death is so final, so irreversible; you long for the one you loved. You can't help dwelling in the past and idealizing the former relationship for a period of time after the death. However, you must accept the challenge of living life in the new way, and form new and different relationships in the here and now. Your own life cycle goes on. You cannot stop. You must keep living, moving, till your cycle is completed.

My hope for you reading this book is to let you know you do have a choice in your pain. To let you know that few people die of grief, except those who *make that choice.* Dying of a "broken heart" to follow a loved one of many years to the grave is a choice.

There is a wonderful story about being an egg or a potato. The woman who told it to me said that she thinks about this story whenever trouble comes. Many years ago when she and her husband lived in India, their six-month-old baby became ill and died. An old Indian gentleman heard of their grief and came to comfort them. He said, "A tragedy like this is similar to being plunged into boiling water. If you are an egg, your affliction will make you hard-boiled and unresponsive. If you are a potato, you will emerge soft and pliable, resilient and adaptable. Which do you want to be?"

My friend says, "It may sound funny to God, but there have been many times when I have prayed, 'Oh, Lord, let me be a potato.'"

An egg or a potato? Hard and cold or warm, alive and adaptable? Many people die a slow and painful death because they choose not to grieve. They remain locked in a shell of unresponsiveness, refusing to feel, and resisting the pain and tests of life.

But remember: if you decide to resist for now, you can always choose tomorrow to feel and experience your grief; to go forward to a newer, stronger you, to a new beginning. You have to clean out the old to make way for the new. The sooner you let go of the pain and the past, the sooner you can start on your new path.

CHAPTER THIRTEEN

CATASTROPHIC DEATHS

Catastrophic deaths are those that are sudden, senseless, unexpected and unjust. The survivors are left with a special set of problems, and the mourning period is prolonged, usually pending legal mandates, court hearings and trials. Frequently the anger stage is extended until legal issues have been resolved. Until recently, with the rise of victim-witness programs, the survivors were left out of the process. Now, in most judicial arenas, victims are kept informed of court dates and can even testify during sentencing if the perpetrator is found guilty.

Murder

Murder is always senseless, reckless and leaves the survivors with many unanswered questions and full of rage. Because murder is such a shock, there is no time to prepare or begin the process of grieving ahead of time. Shock and disbelief are the protective psychological shields that wrap around the survivors for the first several months.

My great aunt and her husband, both in their seventies, were brutally murdered by a neighbor who was drunk and went to their home at 3:30 in the morning demanding money to buy more liquor. When they recognized him and saw that he was already drunk, they refused to give him money. He forced himself into the kitchen and, using a knife, stabbed both of these elderly people to death.

The couple left three adult children and five grandchildren behind. They were all in shock and couldn't believe what had happened. So many lives were affected by the stupidity and violence of his alcoholic attack. My cousins, the murderer's wife and children, and all the extended families suffered. It took three years to get through the legal system, and the murderer is now on death row, still fighting with appeals. The murders occurred in California, where they have a death penalty, but it could be several more years before he is actually executed for his crimes.

When a murderer is caught and taken into custody, it is easier to focus the emotional reaction on the culprit. If the attacker isn't caught, then emotions are more fragmented and may be focused on law enforcement, believing they are not doing enough to find the perpetrator. Other times, the culprit is caught but isn't found guilty of the crime. Consider the O. J. Simpson case: most people believe he was guilty but got off because he could afford high priced and high profile attorneys. In his case, justice may not have been done.

Murder is often an impulsive act of passion done by someone the victim knows or is related to. Frequently, murders are related to drug deals gone sour or organized crime retributions. However, sometimes murder is a random act of senseless killing, as in the Lee Boyd Malvo and John Muhammad shootings of people all over the U.S. They were clearly mentally ill, and the adolescent Lee Boyd was unduly influenced by the older father figure.

In the case of any murder, healing cannot really begin until the legal processes are finished, at least the trial and sentencing. Most victims and families stay stuck in the anger stage until these legal issues are completed.

Support in dealing with the pain and suffering after a murder is tenuous and tentative. Most friends and relatives don't know how to respond. They may worry about prying, or triggering pain, so often they just withdraw. Being left alone may be what some survivors prefer, but others may prefer to talk about what happened. You need to let people know your preferences. Someone who has not experienced this kind of loss will not be able to relate to the profound emotions you are experiencing.

Victims of murder have special support groups because this death they experience is very different than other types of deaths. Only others who have had a similar loss can even begin to fathom what you are going through. Many cities and communities in the United States have such support groups. To find one, call National Victim's Rights Assistance (NOVA). (See Appendix B.)

The Trauma of Victimization

Victims, if they survive, and relatives of victims are both traumatized by a criminal act. The shock leaves them in a state of psychological disruption and disorganization, unable to think clearly or to make decisions. They will feel overwhelmed and devastated by the shock of the action and the emotional pain caused by the crime for a long, long time.

They can't understand why anyone would want to hurt them or someone they love. It is senseless. Their lives may be shattered in a variety of ways. There may be financial loss and physical injury involved. Survivors often suffer post-traumatic stress disorder; for this reason, seeking counseling is a good thing to do.

Frequently, family members are suspected by law enforcement officials, and may be doubly victimized if they are not guilty, as in the Jan Benet Ramsey case in Colorado in 1996. This family was tormented by the Boulder, Colorado Police Department and by the media, which forced them to get their own attorney and finally to move to another city. In high profile cases the media make every detail of the crime public, which often results in a violation of the privacy of the survivors – their mourning and the shock of their traumatic loss have not been respected.

Victim rights groups believe that education of the public about how the criminal justice system works is critical. They believe that the scales of justice have gradually become weighted in favor of the criminal, not the victim, or the family of the victim. If the victim is dead, he or she has no rights or legal standing. Whereas a perpetrator who is arrested may get out on bail, have his trial delayed for over a year, and may go through several years of costly appeals before his final punishment is carried out.

Justice will only be served when those who are not injured by crime feel as indignant as those who are.

Gangs

In the past few decades, there has been a rise of gang related killings. Sometimes "drive-by" shootings cause innocent people to die when a bullet goes astray and misses its intended target. Adolescents, generally boys, who come from families with parents who are often drug users, sellers or alcoholics, form gangs in poor neighborhoods. They are neglected and abused verbally and physically, shamed and blamed, lacking the support and nurturing required to do well in school and see a positive future for themselves. Their self-esteem is non-existent.

With a gang of similar "friends," they form supportive bonds, a new type of family. To join, would-be members often have to prove their courage by passing an induction ritual, which frequently involves committing a crime and not getting caught. Machismo is a cover-up for deep internal feelings of inferiority. If these adolescents were abused as small children, they in turn become abusive. Their internal cannons are loaded and ready to explode, and they are seeking confrontation, putting themselves in harm's way, to either prove their worth or be killed themselves.

Recently, two gang members within the same gang but from different neighborhoods killed two young Hispanic men in increasing intra-gang shootings. In Tucson, for example, gang killings have doubled in the past year, and the problem is getting worse all over the country. Such killings are generally ethnically based.

Experts believe the causes of escalating gang violence include unemployment, high school drop out rates, housing costs, arrest statistics, and gang members who have been arrested "calling the shots" either after they get out or while they are still in prison.

Often, drugs are involved to finance the related criminal behavior. Gang members all have guns and many shootings are the result of young men with guns making very bad impulsive decisions.

Young gang members, if they survive, are headed for a life of crime; they will spend most of their adult lives in and out of prison. What a waste! And what a major social problem, one we have swept under the carpet for too long.

Families of victims of gang violence suffer from the loss of children who either lost their way or who may simply have been in the wrong place at the wrong time. Parents, siblings and other family members will mourn, each in their own way. Family counseling is something to consider to help heal the hole this death leaves in the fabric of the family.

Drunk Drivers

Several years ago a mother whose daughter was killed by a drunk driver started a group called MADD, Mothers Against Drunk Driving. The organization has done a marvelous job of educating the public about not drinking alcohol (or taking drugs) and driving a vehicle. They support families who experience such a death. They have affected legislation and advanced the idea of picking a designated driver when a group is drinking and partying. They have advocated for survivors to participate in the legal processes by being kept informed about hearings and trials. Their work has resulted in longer jail sentences for people whose drunken driving has caused injury or death, and increased funding for programs that educate people about the dangers of driving when drunk.

The grieving process for those who have lost a loved one to a drunk driver is similar in some ways to that experiences by those who have lost someone through murder: in both cases, survivors have to go though the legal system before they really begin the healing process. They are focused on feeling anger toward the person responsible for the death. In cases when the perpetrator isn't caught, they suffer doubly.

They are angry at the judicial system and the unfairness of someone "getting away with murder." They consider the death of their loved one as a murder in which the vehicle was the weapon.

MADD has chapters and support groups all over the country where people can meet and help each other. Many members become activists and go to trials with each other and hold candlelight vigils every year to remember their loved ones whose lives were taken prematurely. There is usually media attention, which keeps the issue before the public consciousness.

The grieving process is especially painful because such deaths are caused by someone else's selfish irresponsibility. Get all the help you can – from counselors, MADD meetings, and from friends and family members.

Other Automobile Accidents

Thousands of people are killed every year in vehicle related accidents as drivers, passengers and pedestrians. These deaths fit the criteria of sudden, senseless, unexpected, and unfair death. Such deaths are different than anticipated deaths, where someone is sick and diagnosed with a terminal illness. Family members, friends and other survivors are not aware of the impending death and don't have the opportunity to begin to mourn and say good-bye before the loss of their loved one.

Automobile accidents are unpredictable. A person gets up in the morning and gets into his or her vehicle with no idea that this is the day he or she will die. It is important to prepare for your death and live every day as if it is your last day. Make every day of your life a quality day. Do good, live well, laugh often and enjoy what you have. Tell the people in your life that you love them; you may never have another chance.

Automobile accidents are the leading cause of death for teenagers, before suicide, which is second. Teenagers are inexperienced drivers. Drivers' education classes in high school help teach them safety rules, but they still die.

Maria's parents, Patricia and James, came to see me for grief counseling after their sixteen-year-old daughter had been killed in an automobile accident two weeks earlier. She had gotten her driver's license three weeks before her death. It was noon on a Saturday when she borrowed the family Bronco and picked up three friends to go to the park to hear a local band play. As she was driving, she was also trying to get a certain station on the car radio. While she was crossing a bridge, she lost control of the car, over-corrected, and the vehicle rolled and pitched over the side of the bridge into the riverbed. All of the youngsters had on seat belts; the passengers were injured but lived. Their daughter Maria was killed.

About 2:00 p.m. the same day, a policeman and two volunteers from the victim witness program came to their door and told them that there had been an accident and that Maria was dead. They were in shock. Distraught and numb with disbelief, they asked where the accident had happened and where Maria was now. The policeman told them she had been taken to the coroner's office and that there would be an autopsy before her body would be released for burial. They offered to get someone to come and stay with them. The victim witness people brought them a teddy bear – an action they considered an insensitive insult, as if a teddy bear could take the place of their beloved daughter.

They were psychologically shattered. They decided to go to the scene of the accident. The car was still there and so was the body of their daughter. When they got to the bridge, a crane was bringing the car up from the riverbed and the Emergency Management Team was bringing Maria's body up over the side of the bridge on a gurney. Her mother ran to the gurney; she wanted to see her daughter.

She was held back and restrained by four policemen who refused to let her go. She was outraged and fought to get free. She is a small woman, only five feet tall. She had lost her shoes and was barefoot on a very hot afternoon on very hot pavement. Her husband was a retired policeman and tried to intervene to get the policemen restraining her to release her and let her go to her daughter's side. They refused, and Maria's body was put into the ambulance to be taken to the corner's office. Now her parents were not only devastated but furious. Patricia sued the city and the police department. It took three years to get the case to trial and she lost. James, a recovering alcoholic, started drinking again and the couple ended up getting a divorce.

In the blink of an eye their lives changed forever, for the worse. What a tragic story for all of them. I know some of you will relate to the tragedy this family experienced.

Other Transportation Accidents: Planes, Trains, Boats, Buses

Random acts of disaster can strike at any moment, and when they do we must accept the event, and adjust to whatever happens. There are many things in our lives that we can control, but some things are completely out of our hands. There were famous international disasters like the sinking of the Titanic, or the Hindenburg bursting into flames while throngs of horrified spectators watched in shock. Almost daily we become aware of airplane crashes, train wrecks and bus accidents in which many people die. These sensational deaths illustrate my point. The whole world mourns.

There are individual personal incidents, such as what happened to one of my clients, whose twenty-six year old grandson was killed in a jet-ski accident when he misjudged and got too close to a dam.

My great grandfather was killed whe he fell off the top of a railroad car while working as a brakeman for a railroad company in 1911. He had a fractured skull and they tried to do brain surgery to save his life. The surgery failed and he died. He left his wife, my great grandmother, a widow with six small children to raise, with no education or viable means to support herself and her family.

Buses have accidents, and when they do, many people can be injured or killed. It is especially tragic when it is a school bus and the passengers are children.

For every death, there are those who are left behind to grieve and mourn the loss of the person they loved. Healing grief after the loss of a loved one is one of life's most painful and challenging times. Yet every one of us will lose people we love; we must honor their memory and go on living until our time comes.

Terrorist Attacks

Killing the maximum number of people with the least risk is the goal of terrorists. In July 2005, 56 people were killed and over 700 were injured when terrorists bombed the London subway system. In Madrid, in March 2004, 191 people were killed and more than 1,700 were injured. The Pan Am Flight 103 airliner bombed in Lockerbie, Scotland killed 270 people – all examples of successful terrorist plots.

On September 11, 2001, groups of terrorists hijacked and crashed four airplanes at critical locations in the United States. Two hit the twin towers in New York City, one hit the Pentagon in Washington D.C., and the other crashed in Pennsylvania after passengers intervened. All of the families who lost a loved one had to grieve to recover; the rest of the people in the United States and in much of the world mourned along with them.

Some families still have not recovered the bodies of their relatives, which makes it difficult for them to finalize their grieving process – to let go and bury their loved one, if not literally, then at least figuratively.

Terrorism is a new concern and a new way of waging war, but terrorist behavior is nothing new. During World War

II, Japanese pilots became kamikaze bombers, flying their planes into United States and Allied war ships and killing themselves in the process, in hopes of sinking the ships. How does someone become seduced into committing suicide for a cause? Such incidents are "no-win" for everyone involved. Everyone becomes a victim.

Zealots who sacrifice their life in the name of nationalism or religious fervor are a mystery to me. Most often, their family members don't know what they are planning to do until the act is competed. They will suffer not only from the loss of a loved one but also the stigma of the act itself, and quite possibly for those who were killed in the terrorist attack. The grief will be painful and complicated for everyone. There may be a desire for vengeance, which just perpetuates the on-going cycle of violence. It must end somewhere – hopefully with you.

War

War is another disastrous way to die. The tragedy of warfare is that politicians who can't resolve their differences through negotiation and mediation sacrifice young and strong young people. And in the process innocent civilians who live in the war zone are killed too. As of this writing, at the end of 2006, it is reported that 665,000 Iraqis have died in the Iraq war.

American military casualties on December 2, 2006 were listed at 2,969 killed, 31,494 wounded. Non-mortal injuries numbered 46,880. This war has now lasted longer than our involvement in World War II, with no end in sight.

These statistics don't include the psychological damage

in the form of Post-Traumatic Stress Disorder and the other difficulties soldiers face when they are reintegrated into civilian life. There was a recent story on the television of a 31-year-old female soldier, a mother of three children, who returned from Iraq. She had trouble adjusting. Within two weeks of her return, she sat on the side of her bed, put a gun to her chest and killed herself.

Boot camp and military training train the enlistees to obey orders at any cost; by emphasizing duty and patriotism, they induce the soldiers, sailors, marines and air force members to be willing to die, and die proudly, for their country. Families who lose a child in warfare may be proud of their child, or they may be outraged and incensed that they get a folded flag in place of their son or daughter.

Motives of the political leaders who declare and engage in war may be hidden or veiled in fear-mongering. There does not seem to be a good reason for the current war in Iraq. Most Americans suspect Iraq's rich oil fields, or its strategic location in the unstable Middle East, are the real underlying motive for waging war in Iraq.

Our involvement in Vietnam also lacked justification, and we withdrew in defeat after the unnecessary deaths of 58,000 Americans. Those who rebelled against the war unfortunately didn't give the troops the support they deserved during the war or after they came home.

War is included in this category of catastrophic deaths because when a son, daughter or spouse goes to war, there are always high hopes that they will return after their term of duty. The sad truth is that many who return are injured physically – or psychologically, in the form of Post-Traumatic Stress

Disorder. Reintegration is difficult, and some never make the adjustment back to civilian life, to the roles of husband or father, wife or mother, daughter or son.

If you have lost a son, daughter or spouse to warfare, you will be called patriotic and praised for making the ultimate sacrifice. This may satisfy you and soothe your grief. But if you disagree with the war, you may feel outraged. Either way, your loss will be terribly painful and you must grieve for it. Look for a support group or talk to a therapist to help you get through the pain.

Abductions and Kidnapping

Many abductions are by parents who are divorced or separated from the person with custody; they take the child or children away from the other parent, sometimes hiding and changing their names, dyeing their hair or otherwise altering their appearance, and attempting to prevent any contact with the other parent.

There are also abductions by strangers, predators who may have contacted the child on the Internet or watched the child play at a playground and tracked his or her activities for awhile, or perhaps discovered the existence of the child while working at the family home as a handyman. When John Walsh's son Adam was abducted and killed, he started America's Most Wanted and raised the public's awareness of child abductions. Now there are photos of missing children on milk cartons, mailed flyers, and television shows.

Walsh has been an advocate for the protection of children; he also started the Amber Alert system, whereby the media immediately announce when a child is missing, giving law enforcement and the public a head start at finding the missing child. Walsh is another example of someone who turned his grief and pain into something positive and productive: helping others in similar situations.

It is important for parents to warn children to be wary of strangers who offer candy, ask for directions, or engage the child in some way that seduces the child to help them. A good idea is to role-play with the child different scenarios that could happen, so your child has a ready response. It is also a good idea to have her wear a whistle to blow if she must walk in secluded places to get home from school or the neighborhood store.

The Internet didn't exist in 1984, when I first wrote this book. Now, it is the predominant way to communicate in most of the world. Sexual predators and child pornographers are rampant on the web, and easily seduce children, and sometimes adults too, depending on their proclivities and the age that stimulates them. Lonely children and teens are prime candidates for perverts. It is critical that parents use parental controls and supervise their children's computer time, keeping track of whom they communicate with.

Child predators are sick people who are frequently obsessed with capturing the child, usually for sexual activity, and they often kill their captives. When I was a little girl, there was a famous case of a child who was abducted, cut into pieces and sent back to the parents in a suitcase. When my parents told me about this, I was horrified and immediately became more careful and wary of strangers. It scared me, which was why they told me: it worked.

If you have had a child kidnapped, you will experience a nightmare of anxiety, fearing the worst until they are found. If they are never found, your nightmare will go on for a long time: you will always be wondering who, when, where and why.

The FBI and other law enforcement officers will most likely be kind and helpful during the search and investigation, but you will be left on your own to deal with the aftermath, whatever the outcome.

Losing a child is one of life's worst losses, but abduction is frequently much worse than other ways of losing a child. Your emotional reserves will be drained, and you will need all the help you can get. Seek it out and ask for it.

Mother Nature

The awesome power of nature can be overwhelming. Human beings are at the mercy of the natural elements and activity on our planet: wildfires, tornadoes, earthquakes, hurricanes, tsunamis, floods, avalanches and volcanic eruptions claim many lives every year. Sometimes entire communities have been wiped out due to a natural disaster. The tsunamis in Southeast Asia in December of 2004 killed 230,000 people in a dozen countries. Many more died later of hunger, and the recovery effort to rebuild the survivors' lives and communities continues. Many people affected by this natural disaster are still without critical infrastructure like roads, power, drainage, and vegetation.

Hurricane Katrina, a category five hurricane, hit New Orleans and the Gulf Coast of the United States in August 2005 with a vengeance, leaving nearly two thousand dead, thousands more homeless, and an estimated $84 billion dollars in damage.

The whole country rallied by donating blood and sending money, clothes, and food to help the relief efforts, but those who lost loved ones have no one to blame and must grieve for those who died. Many survivors experienced multiple losses: their homes, clothes, and personal possessions, many of which are irreplaceable – family photos and personal documents, for example.

Fortunately, with modern technology we sometimes have enough forewarning to evacuate, as the dreaded event gets close. But this is only true of some disasters, and only possible in developed countries where people have better means of communication, a place to go and a way to get there.

These events cause sudden, unexpected deaths, and the grieving process must be done after the fact and after the loss. There will be many others who have gone through the experience with you, so you will have a common sense of loss and you may be able to comfort each other. But for your individual loss, you will feel your own personal pain, and will need to grieve and heal yourself in your own way.

Drug Overdose

One of the saddest ways to lose a child, no matter what age, is from an out-of-control addiction that leads to death by overdose. Barbara came to see me after her 27-year old son died from a drug overdose. He lived in another city and she didn't see him very often, although she talked to him on the phone about once a month. He told her that he had been in a rehabilitation program and that he was looking for a job. She believed him and didn't check any further. She was shocked when she got the call telling her that Mark, her son, was dead.

She was riddled with guilt and self-recrimination about having divorced his abusive father and about not being there for him enough when he needed her. After she had remarried, he had problems adjusting to his new stepfather. He dropped out of school and, after a family argument, moved out of her home and to another city. He was at loose ends and she didn't know how to help him. It took her a long time to deal with her grief and to forgive herself.

If you have lost someone close to you to drugs, either because of an overdose or by other involvement, you may feel guilt or anger at yourself for not being able to prevent the death, especially if you are the parent. The reality is that when children reach their teen-age years, you have taught them all that they will learn from you. When they become adults, they make their own choices and your input will have little effect.

Don't beat yourself up. You will have enough pain to cope with just dealing with having lost your child. Look for some support, and remember: you must go on living for the others in your life who love you and depend on you.

Victimization

There are four main ways that people are victimized. They are physical injuries, financial injuries, emotional injuries, and social injuries.

Physical injuries involve damage to the victim's body: assault, rape, stabbing, gunshot wounds and death. The severity varies, from bruises and cuts to death and everything in between. Not only is the victim involved, but many others are affected also: the victim's family members, the perpetrator, and the family of the perpetrator. If the victim lives, damage may last long after the injuries have healed, in the form of stress related physical symptoms, such as sleep and eating disorders, depression and fear of repetition of the event, nightmares and other Post-Traumatic Stress Disorder symptoms.

Financial injuries involve stealing of money, identity theft, burglary, loss of possessions or property, as in cases of theft or "con jobs." They also involve damage to possessions or property, as in cases of arson, tire-slashing, and the like. Frequently, people who have been victimized in other ways end up with financial injuries, too. Costs may include legal bills, medical care, replacement costs, transportation, childcare, and counseling.

Emotional injuries involve psychological damage, and cause problems such as adjustment disorder, post-traumatic stress disorder, anger management issues, substance abuse, bereavement and other mental health problems that may require therapy.

Social injuries involve a victim being treated insensitively by other people, whether these are fellow workers, law enforcement personnel, the media, family members, neighbors, the legal system, or the clergy. Social injuries happen when victims are not treated with compassion, respect, and sensitivity. One universal complaint is that well-intentioned people often express trite platitudes like, "I know how you feel," or "He's in a better place now," or "It's God's will." Better to listen than give advice presuming it to be helpful. Sometimes a touch says more then words ever can.

CHAPTER FOURTEEN

CAREGIVING

Caregivers are people who accept the role of taking care of a sick or dying person. Some people are cast into this position because they have a child, spouse, sibling, parent or friend who is unable to meet his or her own basic needs: bathing, preparing and eating meals, walking, taking medication as prescribed or doing housekeeping chores. They may or may not embrace the role of caregiver.

Others, including nurses, doctors, hospice volunteers, home health aids and so on, are professional caregivers. When family members are unable or unwilling to care for the disabled relative, an institution may become the home base of the person in need. A caregiver is anyone who assists another person who is ill or disabled and needs some assistance.

The caregiver may live in the same house, in the same neighborhood, in the same town or even in another state. Care may range from small tasks like grocery shopping and picking up prescriptions at the pharmacy to around-the-clock care.

Some families have children who are born with a congenital disease or get sick, even terminally ill, at a young age. Others may have a child who is in an accident and sustains debilitating injuries, subsequently requiring extensive care. Providing this care, or making arrangements for their child's care, means that their lives must change.

Advocacy

Family members have a responsibility to get the best possible care for their loved one, whether he or she is a child, adolescent, adult, elderly parent or sibling. If the person is in an institution like a hospital, assisted living situation, residential facility, or nursing home, family members must check up on the quality of care. If you notice signs that your relative is not receiving adequate care, or if you notice bedsores, bruises or any type of neglect or abuse, go directly to the facility director. And report it to the state licensing board. Beware of excuses from the staff or an attempt to blame the patient. If necessary, move your loved one to another place and monitor the care there.

You are the person responsible for making sure your family member gets the best care possible, especially when she can't act on her own behalf. Elder abuse is rampant in nursing homes, especially those serving low-income folks. Be vigilant! Be assertive! Be sure he is getting the care he deserves.

Parents Caring for Children

Human infants are born the most helpless of any species.

When a baby is born, parents must commit to taking care of and teaching their child from birth until he or she is mature enough to survive without their assistance. Biologically speaking, this is about 12 years old, but socially it is about 18 years old. Children generally leave home to attend college, get a job and live on their own by 18 years old.

We usually think of caregivers as people who take on the role of caring for a sick or dying person. But some children are born with congenital physical problems like spina bifida, heart problems, cystic fibrosis, cerebral palsy, Downs Syndrome, Neimann Pick disease, autism and other problems. Sometimes the problems surface later in life, as happens with childhood cancers and some kinds of mental problems, including schizophrenia, which manifests in adolescence.

Taking care of these children may become emotionally draining, psychologically painful and all-encompassing. Relationships between spouses and other children can be challenged and strained.

If your child is terminally ill, and in and out of the hospital, you will experience an emotional roller coaster with times of crisis and remission. Often such children are more accepting of their own death than parents are, who find it difficult to let them go. This is one of life's most painful situations; it challenges the strongest of emotional bonds, that between parent and child.

After the death you will need to rest and restore your own physical health. Mourning will be an ongoing process, but won't last forever. Attending a support group will be helpful. If there isn't one in your community, start one.

Compassionate Friends supports parents who have lost a child of any age. (See Appendix B.)

When your energy is restored, it is time to refocus on the other loved ones in your life who are still alive and need you.

Children Caring for Parents

As more people live longer and become more frail and dependent as they age, more people require assistance to get through each day. According to the National Alliance for Caregivers (www.caregivers.org) at least 44.4 million American adults provide critical care that allows friends and loved ones with debilitating illnesses to stay in their own homes.

The following information is geared especially to those who are providing care for an elderly person, or a person with a terminal illness.

While each caregiver's situation is unique, there are some common challenges that almost all caregivers face:

- **Less time for personal and family life.** Caregiving takes time, which means less personal time, less leisure time, and less time to spend with other family members.

- **The need to balance caregiver responsibilities and work.** If you have a full time job, you must arrange time off to take the person in your care to doctor's appointments, to be available for emergencies, to talk on the telephone to check up on the person, etc.

- **Financial demands.** Extra gas for trips to the doctor or to buy medical supplies and medications, purchasing special medical equipment, or time lost from work may all be costly and can add up.

- **Physical and emotional stress.** Care-giving takes its toll in emotional and physical stress, leading to exhaustion and sometimes even physical illness for the caregiver.

Critical Issues to Consider in Meeting Needs

Making Decisions

Ideally, the older adult will participate in deciding where to live out the last years of life, to stay in his or her own home or to move to another facility where more supervision and care are available. If a stroke or Alzheimer's or other dementia disease interferes with someone's ability to take care of himself, then the children may need to make some difficult decisions about care and living arrangements for their older parent or parents.

Siblings may have conflicts over making decisions. Old sibling rivalry issues may surface, causing disagreements about distribution of family treasures, selling property, furniture and personal items, either before or after the death. Money is always a trigger issue and needs to be talked about openly. When my mother's mother died, her six children fought over her assets for years and the wounds went so deep that they never completely reconciled. Her oldest son, Tom, was the executor of her estate and the other siblings believed he cheated them. They went their separate ways and all died without ever resolving their differences.

Here are a few suggestions to avoid problems before they get out of control. Do it now — don't wait until there is a crisis. Talk together and work together as a family from the beginning. All relationships take work to run smoothly. Schedule a family conversation and talk about care giving issues and who is willing to do what. Take responsibility yourself; don't assume that someone else will bring it up. Talk about all the issues that you are concerned about, including money and distribution of property, care giving, and options for living arrangements.

Forgive one another for past conflicts; resolve old hurts, and unpack emotional baggage from your childhood. Be courageous and talk about the things that pained you during your childhood. Most often an incident that hurt you was unintentionally inflicted and may not even be remembered by your sibling, and/or can be forgiven now that you are adults.

If you can't resolve these issues alone, then hire a mediator or seek the services of a person experienced in family counseling. If you need one, you may find a mediator at the Family Caregiver Alliance hot line toll-free number. (See Appendix B.) A mediated family session can even be done in a conference call if you live far apart. Your relationships with siblings are potentially the longest of your life, and it is worth the effort to maintain them.

Housing Options

If the person for whom you are caring can move freely around her home and cook and meet most physical needs, she may want to remain in her own home as long as possible.

But realistically, even though she may not like it, she needs to consider the next stage, when she won't be able to function on her own. Now is the time to make decisions about more skilled nursing care.

The person may want to stay in his own home with more help, go into assisted living, try living with relatives, or enter a nursing home. It is best if he makes the decision while he still can – otherwise, others will make it for him.

Important Things to Do Now:

✓ Record Medical History

List medical conditions, doctors, and medications and put this information in a safe place. A magnetic packet on the front of the refrigerator is a good place for paramedics to find the information easily in case of emergency. Consider a Life Alert system in case of a fall or other emergency that would require immediate emergency help, especially if the person you are caring for lives alone.

✓ Make a Personal Support System List

Get a list of the names, addresses and phone numbers of family members, friends, relatives, neighbors, church members, housing managers, accountants, doctors, attorneys and anyone else who is close to the person. Put it in an easy-to-find place.

✓ Create a Financial Profile

List resources – sources of income, including Social Security, pensions, annuities, stocks and bonds, checking and savings accounts, and include account numbers and names, addresses and phone numbers of institutions that hold these documents.

✓ Review Legal Wishes

Encourage a Revocable Living Trust if the estate is over $600,000, or a will if the estate is less. Arrange for an appointment with an attorney to be sure that the documents are legal. At the same time, encourage a durable Power of Attorney and Advanced Directives for end-of-life wishes, so that caregivers are not left powerless to carry out these wishes. Have an attorney review these documents annually for any changes in the law or personal changes.

Find out where important legal documents are kept. Know how to find birth certificates, marriage and divorce documents, Social Security numbers, and deeds to properties, car titles and insurance policies and any other legal papers.

✓   Get Information on Local Services

Find out about delivery of meals, adult day care, home health services, housekeeping help and other services. If you have a local Area Agency on Aging, they can provide information about such services.

Taking Care of Yourself

Many caregivers try to do everything for others and in the process may neglect their own needs and health. If you are the only one providing help and the person you are caring for resists using other services, it can take a serious toll on your own health. It can be an exhausting burden. Here are some tips to help caregivers take care of themselves.

- **Take Care of Your Own Health**

Eat properly, get enough sleep, take time for yourself, and exercise. Schedule personal time for leisure and private time with your own family. Do something special that you enjoy at least once a week.

- **Speak Up When You Need Support or Assistance**

Ask others in the support system for help before you reach the breaking point. Don't try to do everything yourself all alone. Set up and schedule a "circle of friends" as rotating caregivers. I had a friend who was dying of AIDS and his "surrogate family" and friends took turns on a schedule to be with him 24 hours a day for the last four months of his life. The group met once a week to support each other and to get and give updates on his care.

- **Find Out about Services that Help Caregivers**

Case/care management from a social service agency may be able to link your friend or family member to services and benefits available. Adult day care, or respite care, can give you a break when you need it to restore your emotional resources and health.

- **Seek Help or Training to Improve Your Coping Skills**

Local programs, hospitals, hospices, and Area Aging Agencies offer support groups and training for caregivers. Look into these for training and to get support from others facing similar caregiver situations.

End of Life Issues

When the end of life is inevitable and death is predicted to occur within six months, hospice care is a viable option in the United States. Hospice focuses on care, not cure. If hospice care is ordered by a doctor, Medicare pays for it in the United States. Such care includes access to a team of professionals and trained volunteers who are dedicated to providing comfort and relief from pain.

Most hospice care is provided in the home, but hospital care is also available if home care becomes impossible or if the family needs a respite. For people in the final stages of an incurable illness, hospice care helps them and their families stay at home, keep as active as possible, and express and accept feelings of fear, pain, and anger.

For caregivers, hospice teaches them how to provide many types of physical care – to manage practical tasks like giving and charting medications, bathing, preventing bedsores, food preparation and feeding. It teaches them how to deal with stress that the approaching loss creates, and how to give support to each other. It facilitates communication and helps in making final personal and financial decisions. Hospice staff is available 24 hours a day when needed.

Some Diseases Leading to Death

My mother had chronic obstructive pulmonary disease (COPD), a combination of bronchitis and emphysema for several years before she died at 67 years old. She endured gradual increasing difficult breathing problems before she died of congestive heart failure. It was painful to watch her suffering. COPD is the fourth leading cause of death in the United States and affects over 12 million adults.

Cancer, Lou Gehrig's Disease (ALS), multiple sclerosis, heart disease, Parkinson's disease, and diabetes are some other causes of death that can be either fast or slow and lingering; all are likely to worsen as the person ages.

One benefit to being a caregiver to someone with a terminal illness is that you and the dying person can, if you both wish, talk about life and death together. There can be time to clean up the business of life – to get financial matters in order, make amends, clean up ruptured relationships and talk about after-death issues like burial, cremation preferences, memorial services and so on.

Quality of Life

As people live longer, there are issues that need to be considered and decisions that need to be made about housing, finances, transportation, family, health care and so on. Most people today become very frail by the time they reach their eighties. It is more difficult for them to take care of themselves.

One option is to go into a residential facility that provides a continuum of care. Residents usually must be ambulatory before they are accepted. Supervision and skilled nursing care are available and may be increased as they need more help.

Community meals are provided, trips are planned, shopping is organized, and cleaning and laundry services are available, all of which allows residents to be independent as long as possible. This is a choice many older people are making in the United States, and some places in Europe, if they can afford it. For those who prefer not to live with one of their children, or those who have no children, it is a good option.

There are for-profit and not-for-profit facilities available. A specific church usually operates the not-for-profit ones.

The Future

Without a reliable crystal ball, it is difficult to accurately predict the future. Modern medical research promises to deliver better health to the aging population. Stem cell research can regenerate worn out organs, like the pancreas for diabetics, joints and cartridge for arthritis-sufferers, and even livers and hearts. Cures for Parkinson's disease and other autoimmune diseases may be discovered sometime within the next 50 to 100 years.

We already have the remarkable life-extending transplant capability for many people with failing hearts, lungs, livers, eyes, and other organs.

The human organism is capable of living to 120 years. However, when people are asked if they *want* to live that long, most people say no, unless the quality of life for elderly people were to improve significantly.

Old age today brings many discomforts, including osteo-arthritis for almost everyone over the age of 60, which especially affects any place an old injury occurred. We have outlived the viable use of our reproductive organs, so they create problems and often need to be removed; we are all at higher risk for cancers in these parts. Breast cancer, ovarian and uterine cancer, and prostate cancer are common as we age.

We are still victims of the wear-and-tear of biological aging. Our immune systems don't function sufficiently to protect us with certainty against the next disease lurking around the corner.

We are also affected by lifestyle choices like smoking. Until the 1970's, who knew that this fashionable habit would eventually lead to a slow and tormented death from lung disease, or a fast one from heart disease?

What does alcohol and caffeine do to our bodies? What about preservatives, pesticides, and air pollution?

Just Do the Best You Can

Here are my final words of wisdom:

Live well.

Laugh often.

Love with all your heart.

Give back.

Help others.

Don't judge others.

Leave a legacy behind so someone knows you were here.

Overcome the obstacles life puts in your path; let them be your teachers. Learn from them.

Die in peace knowing you did the best you could do with the time you had here on earth.

APPENDIX A

Here are suggestions for the friends and relatives of the grieving survivor.

Get in touch. Telephone. Speak either to the mourner or to someone close and ask when you can visit and how you might help. Even if much time has passed, it's never too late to express your concern.

Say little on an early visit. In the initial period (before burial), your brief embrace, your press of the hand, your few words of affection and feeling may be all that is needed.

Avoid clichés and easy answers. "He had a good life," "He is out of pain," and "Aren't you lucky that...," are not likely to help. A simple "I'm sorry" is better. Likewise, spiritual sayings can even provoke anger unless the mourner shares the faith that is implied. In general, *do not attempt to minimize the loss.*

Be yourself. Show your own natural concern and sorrow in your own way and in your own words.

Keep in touch. Be available. Be there. If you are a close friend or relative, your presence might be needed from the beginning. Later, when close family may be less available, anyone's visit and phone call can be very helpful.

Attend to practical matters. Discover if you might be needed to answer the phone, usher in callers, prepare meals, clean the house, care for the children, etc. This kind of help lifts burdens and creates a bond. It might be needed well beyond the initial period, especially for the widowed.

Encourage others to visit or help. Usually, one visit will overcome a friend's discomfort and allow him or her to contribute further support. You might even be able to schedule some visitors, so that everyone does not come at once in the beginning or fails to come at all later on.

Accept silence. If the mourner doesn't feel like talking, don't force conversation. Silence is better than aimless chatter. The mourner should be allowed to lead.

Be a good listener. When suffering spills over in words, you can do the one thing the bereaved needs above all else at that time: you can listen. Is he emotional? Accept that. Does he cry? Accept that too. Is he angry at God? God will manage without your defending him. Accept whatever feelings are expressed. Do not rebuke. Do not change the subject. Be as understanding as you can be.

Do not attempt to tell the bereaved how he feels. You can ask (without probing), but you cannot know, except as he tells you. Everyone, bereaved or not, resents an attempt to describe his feelings. To say, for example, "You must feel relieved now that he is out of pain," is presumptuous. Even to say, "I know just how you feel," is questionable. Learn from the mourner; do not instruct him.

Do not probe for details about the death. If the survivor offers information, listen with understanding.

Comfort children in the family. Do not assume that a seemingly calm child is not sorrowing. If you can, be a friend to whom feelings can be confided and with whom tears can be shed. In most cases, incidentally, children should be left in the home and not shielded from the grieving of others.

Avoid talking to others about trivia in the presence of the recently bereaved. Prolonged discussion of sports, weather, or the stock market, for example, is resented, even if done purposely to distract the mourner.

Allow the "working through" of grief. Do not whisk away clothing or hide pictures. Do not criticize seemingly morbid behavior. Young people may repeatedly visit the site of the fatal accident. A widow may sleep with her husband's pajamas as a pillow. A young child may wear his dead sibling's clothing.

Write a letter. A sympathy card is a poor substitute for your own expression. If you take time to write of your love for and memories of the one who died, your letter might be read many times and cherished, possibly into the next generation.

Encourage the postponement of major decisions until after the period of intense grief. Whatever *can* wait *should* wait.

In time, gently draw the mourner into quiet, outside activity. He may not have the initiative to go out on his own.

When the mourner returns to social activity, treat him as a normal person. Avoid pity – it destroys self-respect. Simple understanding is enough. Acknowledge the loss, the change in his life, but don't dwell on it.

Be aware of needed progress through grief. If the mourner seems unable to resolve anger or guilt, for example, you might suggest a consultation with a clergy member or other trained counselor.

A final thought: Helping must be more than following a few rules. Especially if the bereavement is devastating and you are close to the bereaved, you may have to give more time, more care, *more of yourself* than you imagined. And you will have to perceive the *special needs* of your friend or family member and creatively attempt to meet those needs. Such commitment and effort may even save a life. At the least, you will know the satisfaction of being truly and deeply helpful.

-Amy Hillyard Jensen

Appendix B
Resources and Organizations

1. American Adoption Congress, Box 42730, Washington, D.C. 20015. Website: www.americanadoptioncongress.org Promotes adoption reform through further study, research, and teaching knowledge of adoptions and related social psychological issues in the U.S.

2. American Foundation for Suicide Prevention (AFSP) Website: www.theovernight.org Founded in 1987 to fund research in suicide prevention. A fascinating website loaded with information, including a discussion of euthanasia and assisted suicide.

3. The Compassionate Friends, P.O. Box 3696, Oak Brook, IL 60522. Toll-free telephone: 877-969-0010 Website: www.compassionatefriends.org Non-profit and non-denominational, informal self-help organization open to parents who have experienced the death of a child of any age. Offers physical and emotional help to bereaved parents, grandparents and siblings.

4. Concern for Dying 250 W. 57th Street, New York, NY 10107 Telephone: 212-246-6973 This agency will provide legal information about Living Wills and Durable Powers of Attorney for Health Care, as applicable in your own state.
Another resource is the *American Association of Retired Persons.* For a single, free copy of the *Health Care Power of Attorney* booklet, please send a postcard with your name and address to:

AARP Fulfillment (Stock No. D13895)
1909 K Street, N.W.
Washington, D.C. 20049

5. Sudden Infant Death Syndrome (SIDS) Network
Assists bereaved parents who have lost a child to SIDS; works with families and professionals in caring for high risk infants. Supports research for public education of SIDS and related issues.

National SIDS Alliance, 1314 Bedford Ave., Suite 210, Baltimore, MD 21208. Telephone: (800) 221-7437. Fax: (410) 653-8709

National Sudden Infant Death Syndrome Resource Center (NSRC), 2070 Chain Bridge Road Suite 450, Vienna, VA 22182. Telephone: 703-821-8955. Fax: 703-821-2098. E-mail: info@circsol.com

6. Mothers Against Drunk Driving (MADD)
Website: www.madd.org
A non-profit group with regional and state groups. Acts as the voice of the victim in drunk driving accidents. Supports Highway Patrol programs and state and federal legislation for reform of laws on drunk driving. Counsels victims. MADD's mission is to stop drunk driving, support the victims of this violent crime and prevent underage drinking.

7. Parents of Murdered Children (POMC)
National POMC, 100 East Eighth Street, Suite B-41, Cincinnati, Ohio 45202. Toll Free: 888-818-POMC.
Website: www.pmoc.com
This is a self-help organization of parents whose children have been murdered, but its purpose is to provide support and

assistance to all survivors of homicide victims while working to create a world free of murder. Provides information about the criminal justice system as it pertains to survivors of a homicide victim. 35 local groups — or start your own. Publishes quarterly newsletter.

8. *The Center for Social Gerontology (TCSG)*
2307 Shelby Avenue, Ann Arbor, Michigan 48103
Telephone: 734-665-1126. Website: www.tcgs.org
TCSG's mission is to help society adapt to the dramatic increase in the numbers of old and very old, and to insure that older persons at all socio-economic and health levels are able to meet their needs and use their talents and abilities in a changing society. Lobbies for the aging of America in formulating social policies and programs with policy makers.

9. *Elder Decisions,* 175 Bedford Street Suite #5,
Lexington, Ma 02420. Telephone: 617-621-1588
Website: www.elderdecisions.com
Changes in people's needs and roles as they age can impose new stresses on elders and their loved ones. Faced with these challenges, many families seek help to develop new ways of coping with evolving relationships and changing realities. They provide mediation as an opportunity for the elder and all concerned members of the family to participate in creating a thoughtful plan for the future. They facilitate conflict resolution between siblings and other family members.

10. *Family Caregiver Alliance,* Toll-free telephone:
800-445-8106. E-mail: www.info@caregiver.org
Website: www.caregiver.org
Offers state-by-state information by telephone and by e-mail

to families making caregiver decisions. Monitors public policy state by state and gives resources for each state.

11. National Hospice & Palliative Care Organization (NHPCO), 1700 Diagonal Road, Suite 625, Alexandria, Virginia 22314. Telephone: 703-837-1500. Fax: 703-837-1233

12. Instituto Mexicano de Tanatologia A.C.,
Av. Insurgentes Sur No. 2047, 1er piso, Office No. 4, San Angel Delegacion Alvaro, Obregon, Mexico DF 01000. Telephone: 011-52-5662-1250. E-Mail: contacto@thanatologia.org.mx Website: www.tanatologia.org.mx

This remarkable institute educates doctors, nurses, and other health care providers in Mexico and all over Latin America about issues related to death and dying. Additionally, they seek to provide services to families with a terminally ill or sick member. They use this book as required reading for all of their students.

13. The Neptune Society
Telephone: 1-800-637-8863
Website: www.neptunesociety.com
Provides cremation and burial at sea. Has offices in 11 states.

14. Celestis Foundation
Website: www.memorialspaceflights.com
Memorial Spaceflights place a symbolic portion of cremated remains into Earth orbit, onto the lunar surface, and into deep space.

About the Author:

Nancy O'Connor, Ph.D., is a psychologist with 20 years of clinical experience. She has served as a faculty member at the University of Oregon and the University of Arizona. She was the Director of both The Grief and Loss Center and La Mariposa Counseling Services, Inc. in Tucson, Arizona until her retirement in 1998. She is a consultant to various government agencies, social service agencies, mental health agencies, and private businesses. She conducts workshops and seminars on grief, bereavement, loss, and growth and development, both nationally and internationally.

Books and CD's by Dr. O'Connor may be ordered from:
www.lamariposapress.com

La Mariposa Press

Telephone: 520-615-1244

Fax: 520-299-4840

E-mail: DocNanO@aol.com.

Or write to: 1990 E. Campbell Terrace
          Tucson, Arizona 85718-5952